The Fiber for Life Cookbook

Bryanna Clark Grogan

Book Publishing Company
Summertown, Tennessee

© 2002 Bryanna Clark Grogan   Photos © 2002 Book Publishing Company
Cover design: Warren Jefferson, Cynthia Holzapfel, Michael Cook
Interior design: Gwynelle Dismukes   Photography: Warren Jefferson

Pictured on the cover:
Upper right: Lee's Black-Eyed Pea Salad, p. 81
Lower left: Fiber-Rich Chocolate Chip Cookies, p.171, Biscotti di Prato, p. 170

Published by
Book Publishing Company
P.O. Box 99
Summertown, TN 38483
1-888-260-8458   www.bookpubco.com

Printed in Canada
ISBN13 978-1-57067-134-0   ISBN10 1-57067-134-6

14 13 12 11 10   2 3 4 5 6 7 8 9 0

Grogan, Bryanna Clark, 1948-
  The fiber for life cookbook / by Bryanna Clark Grogan.
      p. cm.
  ISBN 1-57067-134-6
  1. High-fiber diet--Recipes. 2. Low-fat diet--Recipes. I. Title.
  RM237.6 .G764 2002
  641.5'63--dc21

                         2002008617

Book Publishing Co. is a member of Green Press Initiative. We chose to print this title on paper with postconsumer recycled content and processed chlorine free, which saved the following natural resources:

9 trees   256 pounds of solid waste
4,253 gallons of water   3 million BTU of net energy
883 pounds of greenhouse gases

For more information visit: www.greenpressinitiative.org. Savings calculations from the Environmental Defense Paper Calculator <www.edf.org/papercalculator>

g green
  press
  INITIATIVE

TABLE OF CONTENTS

DEDICATION: This book is lovingly dedicated to my mother, Eve (Marie Evelyn) Tonge Urbina, who gave me a taste for good, health-giving foods.

INTRODUCTION

How Can Fiber Be Gourmet?

This was the challenge I set for myself when I started to write this book. I was a young wife and mother in the 1960s and '70s, so I remember well the heavy brown "natural food" recipes of the day. We were on the right track—we knew that the food we had grown up on was not necessarily the most conducive to good health. We hadn't quite figured out the ins and outs of cooking with whole grains, and we had no idea that using lots of fat might not be such a great thing. We shunned white sugar, or any sugar, like a plague—although we used plenty of honey—and we used butter with abandon! Since no one had ever heard of whole wheat pastry flour, we used regular whole wheat bread flour, so our cakes and biscuits were a little on the heavy side. Brown rice was served with just about everything. Whole wheat pastas were seldom made from durum semolina wheat, so they were dark in color and heavy and pasty in flavor and texture. Many natural foods cooks believed that salt was poison, so our whole grain offerings were often flat-tasting.

But we persevered. We explored the food of other cultures, which gave us our best recipes, such as tabbouleh, hummus, and other dishes that eventually became standard natural foods fare. Since then, we've incorporated exotic vegetables and learned to cook with less fat, but most of us have abandoned our purist principles and have permitted some of the dreaded "white" foods to creep back into our cupboards and onto our plates. So it's a propitious time to become aware of fiber once again.

Our grandmothers really knew a thing or two when they urged us to get our "roughage," employ "Nature's broom," and stay "regular." It's not something we talk about at cocktail parties, but just about every magazine you read these days has something to say about fiber and how it can help you lose weight, prevent cancer, reduce insulin levels, and prevent heart disease. The problem is that most people don't think they'll like fiber-rich foods, and they don't know how to make fiber taste good.

In this book, I present high-fiber recipes that really work, that you will want to eat, and that you will want to serve to your family and friends. I refused to have any recipe in this book that I didn't like a lot.

The recipes here are strictly vegetarian—vegan, in fact, calling for no animal products of any kind—but this may be a boon to meat-eaters, in light of the fact that they are urged by nutritionists to eat a few vegetarian meals a week and to eat more vegetables and grains. The recipes in this book can help you do just that without feeling deprived in any way.

I hope you will learn from this book, have a bit of an adventure, and enjoy some really good eating!

Bryanna Clark Grogan
Denman Island, B.C.
Canada

FIBER: WHAT'S IT ALL ABOUT?

British medical scientist Dr. Denis Burkitt worked for 20 years as a surgeon in Africa, where he noticed that native Africans eating their traditional diet almost never suffered from diseases that were extremely common in industrial societies in the West. For many years after leaving Africa, he studied the worldwide geographical distribution of these common diseases. He found strong evidence, confirmed in many medical studies since then, that dietary factors, especially the absence of dietary fiber, played a role in these diseases.

Dr. Burkitt likened fiber to the skeleton of the plant. The skeleton, or cell walls, he likened to a carton or container. The contents are the nutrients. Much attention has been paid to the contents, Dr. Burkitt said, but little to the cell walls. All of the attention was focused on the proteins, fats, carbohydrates, vitamins, and minerals that are absorbed by the body. Fiber contains none of these things, contributes none of the benefits of these things, performs none of the jobs which these substances perform in our bodies, so it was pretty much ignored, except as Grandma's proverbial "broom" for the intestines.

The outside layers of seeds, fruits, legumes, and other foods can also be thought of as cartons or containers. They are removed and discarded with refining, whether it is in the milling and production of white flour, the extraction of sugar from beet or cane, or the extraction of oil from seeds, cereals, and nuts. Although some fiber remains in certain foods, the discarding of these outside layers in so many of our common foods eliminates most of this important substance from the diets of most North Americans.

Fiber is a catch-all term for literally hundreds of different substances, all with importance to our health. At one time, fiber was equated almost entirely with cellulose and lignin (the woody parts of plants)—what we used to call crude fiber and now call insoluble fiber. Left out are other important constituents of fiber, the soluble fibers (see sidebar on page 18). All of these constituents play their part, both in the construction of a plant and in terms of our health. The composite term for all of these fibers is dietary fiber.

For thousands of years, humans have been aware that roughage (which referred primarily to insoluble fiber) prevents constipation and its related problems. Until quite recently, we assumed that the beneficial effect of fiber came from its ability to absorb water like a sponge. But now we know that bran fiber, the most effective dietary fiber for treating constipation, absorbs water very badly! What it does, however, is nurture aerobic bacteria and yeasts which create a soft bulk that moves intestinal contents along easily, adjusts alkalinity and acidity, and detoxifies chemicals in the gastrointestinal system that can cause cancer, among other problems.

If fiber is missing from the diet, the opposite effect will take place—anaerobic bacteria take over and cancer-producing toxins are produced in the gut by bacteria that flourish in a fiber-deficient system.

So, it's not just constipation we're talking about, troublesome as that is. Constipation is a precursor of, or the cause of, many other common complaints and life-threatening conditions as diverse as diverticular disease (a common and painful disease of the colon), large bowel cancer, colon cancer and breast cancer, gallstones, hiatus hernia, appendicitis, heart disease, varicose veins, obesity, diabetes, and hemorrhoids, many of which are all but unknown in peoples whose diets are high in fiber.

HOW FIBER CAN DEFEAT DISEASE

Constipation

Although it's not a topic for polite conversation, we've all experienced it. In rural communities of the Third World, where minimally processed, high-carbohydrate foods comprise the majority of the diet, intestinal transit time—the time it takes food to travel through and out of your digestive system—is about 1½ days.

In Western countries, in healthy young adults, transit time is twice that, and in the elderly, it can be as long as two weeks! But constipation isn't just about the time it takes to process your food. Those Third World residents mentioned above have sometimes three to four times as much stool by weight as we do, and that stool is soft, compared to the typically hard stool of a Westerner. All of these things are elements of constipation.

A diet rich in dietary fiber is the easiest way to prevent this condition. Drinking a lot of water will not, in itself, make any difference, unless it is combined with a high-fiber diet. Without fiber, water will simply be absorbed from the bowel to be excreted in urine.

Diverticular Disease

About one in ten people over forty and one in three over sixty in Western countries will have diverticular disease. It is now recognized as a direct result of constipation. Diverticular disease is the development of small pouches in the wall of the colon. It can be quite painful. When the stool is soft and volumi-nous, as mentioned above, it is easily propelled along through your intestines. When it is hard and firm, it becomes resistant to movement and the bowel-wall muscle has to work very hard to eliminate it. The muscle thickens in an attempt to increase its efficiency, making increased pressure in the bowel. The increased pressure can force these small pouches (diverticula) out through the bowel lining. In the past, doctors thought that a high-fiber diet would irritate the lining of the bowel. Fortunately, we now know that the opposite is true.

But a high-fiber diet does not cure the problem once you have it (although it can prevent the need for surgery), so prevention is important. Adopt a high-fiber diet BEFORE you develop this common ailment!

Appendicitis

Appendicitis is an inflammation of the appendix, a blind-ended tube about two inches long that opens into the large intestine, called the caecum. The infection is caused by blockage of the cavity of the appendix, often by a hard lump of fecal matter only the size of a pea, and usually requires swift surgical removal to prevent even more dangerous infections. This will happen only when the stool is hard and dry. Another cause of blockage can be a muscle spasm caused by extraordinary efforts of the muscle to push out hard fecal matter, which can close off the wider cavity of the appendix.

Dr. Burkitt noticed that appendicitis was a rarity among his African patients. But when Africans moved to Britain or other Western countries to study, or when, for example, African troops ate British Army rations, they were more likely to develop appendicitis. Studies in Western countries confirmed that those who consistently ate whole wheat bread rather than white bread had a much lower risk of developing appendicitis. Keeping the contents of the bowel soft is the best safeguard against appendicitis.

Hiatus Hernia

This describes a condition in which the top of the stomach is pushed up into the thoracic cavity. About one in five North Americans will have this condition, even if it causes no greater symptoms than heartburn (both heartburn and hiatus hernia are uncommon in Third World countries). This protrusion is caused by straining to pass stool. When the stomach has been pushed up into the thorax, the closure of the lower end of the gullet (which acts like a valve), becomes less efficient, allowing acid from the stomach to enter. This can cause what is known as acid reflux, which can cause a burning sensation in the esophagus and eventually erode it. If left untreated, surgery may be necessary. Adopting a high-fiber diet can reduce straining and may reduce the need for surgery.

Varicose Veins

Varicose veins? What do they have to do with fiber? Veins near the surface of the legs are susceptible to swelling and distortion because they have less support around them than the deeper veins, which are surrounded by muscle. People in Western industrialized nations are afflicted with this condition far more often than those in Third World countries. We often blame varicose veins on childbearing, but in poorer countries with higher birth rates, varicose veins aren't as common in women as those in affluent countries with lower birth rates. The exact cause is not known, but it is widely thought to be caused by damage to the veins from abdominal straining, which puts pressure on the veins. The pressure forces blood through the leg veins, eventually stretching them so much that the valves cannot function properly. The weight of the extra blood eventually distorts the veins.

Hemorrhoids

According to Dr. Burkitt, hemorrhoids know no national boundaries, but they are much less common in Third World countries (one out of every two North Americans over 50 will have them). True hemorrhoids are cushions of blood vessels that surround the upper end of the anal canal to help prevent fecal matter from escaping. These are present from birth. Abdominal straining, caused by constipation, will cause these cushions to swell and literally be pushed outside the anus, a condition called prolapse.

Most people who suffer from hemorrhoids can be treated simply with a high-fiber diet. This can greatly reduce the need for surgery, and can, of course prevent the problem in the first place.

Gallstones

Gallstones are exceedingly rare among Africans, yet the removal of the gallbladder is one of the most frequent surgical operations in Western countries. The gallbladder is a small sac that stores bile; it is attached to a tube that carries bile to the duodenum, where it is used to digest fatty foods. Gallstones develop in people whose bile has the wrong proportions of cholesterol and solvent bile salts. Gallstones can cause obstructions in a couple of locations, and an obstruction can result in severe complications, including high fever, severe abdominal pain, vomiting, and jaundice. Chronic inflammation can cause the gallbladder to cease function.

What role does fiber play in all this? Dietary fiber binds with cholesterol and reduces its chances of absorption. It also binds bile salts in fecal matter so that more are eliminated and less are returned to the liver. The combination of these actions reduces the amount of cholesterol reaching the liver and increases the need for liver cholesterol to turn into bile salts, which may decrease liver cholesterol.

Heart Disease and High Blood Pressure

Cholesterol, of course, plays a role in heart disease, the most common cause of death in the Western world, among women as well as men. It is rare where people work hard physically and eat a simple, natural diet. While there are several protective measures you can take to protect yourself from heart disease, there is conclusive evidence that eating soluble fiber, such as that in oat bran, flaxseeds, soybeans, and other legumes can lower the "bad" LDL cholesterol. Soluble fiber apparently binds some of the body's cholesterol and carries it out of the body as waste. Eating more whole grains, fruits, vegetables, nuts, and seeds may also leave little room in the diet for fatty meats, cheeses, and refined foods, which also are known to elevate cholesterol.

Elevated blood pressure (hypertension) is often called the "silent killer" because it can go unnoticed for years, causing irreversible damage to some vital organs in the meantime. Research shows that people who eat high-fiber diets have lower blood pressures than those who consume low-fiber diets. It is well-known by researchers that, in countries where high-fiber diets are the norm, blood pressure does not rise with age, as is common in the Western world.

Obesity

People who are overweight are more at risk for elevated blood pressure and diabetes than those who are not. Obesity appears to more than double the risk for heart attack; among women with coronary artery disease, 70 percent are significantly overweight.

A high-fiber diet can help you lose weight. Fiber is the only constituent of our daily diet that contains no calories, so eating a high-fiber diet may decrease the calories absorbed by a small amount that may be significant enough over time to cause weight loss. Whole foods require more chewing, as a rule, which may help you to eat more slowly and feel full sooner. Whole foods are also more satisfying and filling than refined foods, and this feeling of fullness may prevent you from eating empty calories.

Although obesity is cited as a risk factor for both heart disease and high blood pressure, it may be more a matter of where the pounds are situated on your body than how many. It has been known since 1956 that women who carry excess weight around their middles, rather than on their hips, thighs, and buttocks, are more vulnerable to high blood pressure, high cholesterol, and diabetes. This has been confirmed by many other studies since then, leading one researcher to suggest that heart disease should be compared in "pear-shaped" versus "apple-shaped" people, not men and women.

The pot-belly, no-waistline, male-pattern apple profile (as opposed to the more feminine, fat-below-the-waist pear shape) affects insulin and fatty acid production, which predisposes us to coronary artery disease. Abdominal obesity causes fatty acids and triglycerides to be "poured" into major veins from the abdominal fat cells and settle as plaque in our blood vessels.

A waist-to-hip ratio greater than 0.8 indicates cardiac risk. To figure out your ratio, divide your waist measurement by your hip measurement. A low-fat, high-fiber plant-based diet and regular exercise, including weight training or resistance training, can help you lose weight. You may not ever be what you consider slim, but you will most likely reduce your waist-to-hip ratio, and become stronger and fitter and generally healthier in the bargain.

Diabetes

Non-insulin-dependent diabetes, or Type 2, diabetes mellitus, the most common form of diabetes, is caused by the body's inability to burn off dietary sugars (to simplify it enormously). The liver converts the sugars from carbohydrate foods into glucose, a form of sugar that is used for energy in the body. The levels of glucose are controlled by the hormone insulin, which is produced by the pancreas. If there isn't enough insulin, or if the insulin isn't working properly, the glucose may go out of control (called hyperglycemia, or excess blood sugar). If diabetes isn't treated, serious damage may occur to vital organs.

Fiber can help diabetes-prone individuals in a number of ways. First, it helps to control obesity, because the more fat the body has, the more insulin it needs to control glucose. Secondly, fiber inhibits or slows down the release of sugars contained in foods—particularly the soluble fibers, such as the pectin in apples and gums found in oats and beans—and slows down the absorption of glucose from the small intestine. These same viscous fibers help rid the body of built-up excess cholesterol, which forms plaque in the arteries. This is a boon to diabetics, who are at greater risk for stroke and heart disease.

Diabetics used to be prescribed a low-carbohydrate, high-fat diet in order to keep the intake of sugars as low as possible, but now diabetics are urged to adopt a low-fat, largely plant-based diet high in complex (unrefined) carbohydrates—vegetables, fruits, beans,

and whole grains. Some studies have shown that adults with insulin-dependent or Type 1 diabetes may lower their insulin requirements by an average of 40 percent if they adopt this type of high-fiber diet. Adults with non-insulin-dependent (Type 2) have even more dramatic results. (Be sure to work with your doctor when changing your diet, if you have diabetes.)

Cancer

I am always cautious when reporting that any food can help prevent or treat cancer, so I would like to quote directly from a paper called "Health implications of dietary fiber—Position of ADA" (The American Dietetic Association, *Journal of the American Dietetic Association*, 1997;97:1157-1159.)

"Correlation studies that compare colorectal cancer incidence or mortality rates among countries with estimates of national dietary fiber consumption suggest that fiber intake may be protective against colon cancer. When results of 13 case-control studies of colorectal cancer rates and dietary practices were pooled, it was concluded that the results provided substantive evidence that intake of fiber-rich foods is inversely related to risks of both colon and rectal cancer. It is estimated that the risk of colorectal cancer in the U.S. population could be reduced by about 31 percent if fiber intake from food sources were increased by an average of about 13g a day..."

You may have seen the front-page stories that announced, "2 Fiber Studies Find No Benefit for the Colon." Here are some comments by cancer experts about the studies that prompted these headlines:

"Did they use a high enough dose of fiber?" asked John Baron, colon cancer expert at Dartmouth College in Hanover, NH. "Did the study start too late in life? What if the participants didn't really eat as much fiber as the researchers told them to?"

"The recurrence of polyps is a ten-year process," stated David Alberts, who heads a new study called the Wheat Bran Trial.

"The intervention trials lasted three or four years. It could be that only long-term fiber use is associated with a reduction in polyps. It might take a lifetime of higher fiber intake, not just the two or three years' worth required in the recent studies, to prevent colon cancer," said Joanne Slavin, Ph.D., R.D., professor in the department of food sciences at the University of Minnesota.

There is so much data linking high fiber with lowered colon-cancer risk that we simply can't ignore. As John D. Potter, M.D., Ph.D., from the Fred Hutchinson Cancer Research Center said in an editorial in the *New England Journal of Medicine*, "We have barely begun."

And, as the ADA paper stated, epidemiological studies have long shown that populations who eat more fiber have fewer incidences of colon cancer. And other studies have shown that risk of this cancer decreased as fiber was increased in the diet. The theory is that fiber, by bulking up the stools, dilutes the concentrations of toxins passing through the gut, possibly decreasing the opportunity for them to damage cells in the colon or to be absorbed into the bloodstream. Fiber may also decrease the time that toxins stay in the intestines, reducing the opportunity for cell damage. Some researchers believe that the natural bacteria that is encouraged by a high-fiber diet discourages the growth of cancer.

And what about the claims that a high-fiber diet can prevent breast cancer? These claims have also been controversial. But recent research suggest that insoluble fiber binds to estrogen—an important breast cancer risk factor—reducing estrogen blood levels. A study published in the *American Journal of Clinical Nutrition* showed that women who doubled their intake of fiber from 15 to 30 grams a day had significantly lower estrogen levels after two months.

Epidemiological studies show a correlation between high fiber intake and lowered risk of breast and prostate cancer, but scientists aren't sure whether there are other factors present, such as lowered fat, higher intake of antioxidants and phytochemicals, or higher levels of phytoestrogens (particularly from soyfoods).

Nevertheless, there is enough evidence to suggest that you have nothing to lose by adopting a high-fiber diet as part of a cancer-prevention plan. It has so many other proven benefits that it can't hurt!

How Much Fiber Do We Need?

The World Health Organization recommends an intake of 27-40 grams of fiber a day for most adults. Most health experts would like us to eat 40 grams a day as a protective dose, but usually recommend only 30 grams because they don't think that the average American can contrive to eat 40 grams a day! That average meat-eating North American eats only about 15 grams of fiber a day—and many do not even come close to that.

The average ovo-lacto-vegetarian consumes 30-40 grams a day, and the average vegan consumes 40-50 grams a day, so it's clear that eating animal products (which have no fiber) pushes fiber-rich plant foods out of the diet.

How can I get all the fiber I need?

It's actually very easy! Rather than taking the prescriptive approach (i.e., keep on eating what you are eating now and add 1 tablespoon of bran to each meal, which would only give you an extra 6 grams or so a day), I recommend the whole foods approach. Experts don't advise you to eat your fiber naked (in supplements, or simply by adding bran to your food) because you miss out on so many valuable nutrients. Instead, learn to cook with, and enjoy, the myriad of delicious fiber-rich plant foods at our disposal.

☆ Fiber Superstars ☆

Below is my personal list of fiber superstars (you can see why beans are recommended!). These foods have 4.5 mg or more of dietary fiber in a reasonable serving, but that doesn't mean that you should ignore other plant foods that have less fiber; they would contribute small amounts of fiber to add to your daily total, plus vitamins, minerals, and antioxidants.

Can you get too much fiber? Well, you can get too much of just about anything, I suppose, but it's highly unlikely in our modern world! Some

☆ FIBER SUPERSTARS ☆

Food	Fiber (g)	Food	Fiber (g)	Food	Fiber (g)
1 large apple	4.5	1 cup chickpeas	6.0	1 cup zucchini	6.0
4 artichoke hearts	4.5	2 tablespoons dried coconut	6.8	¼ cup pearled barley	8.0
8 ounces baked beans in tomato sauce	16.0	½ cup cream-style corn	5.0	¼ cup dry kamut or spelt	8.0
1 cup black beans	16.0	3 dried figs	10.5	¼ cup steel-cut oats	5.0
1 cup white beans	16.0	1 cup cooked greens	8.0	⅓ cup uncooked oat groats	6.0
1 cup baby limas or butter beans	7.4	⅔ cup brown lentils	5.5	⅓ cup uncooked quinoa	6.0
1 cup kidney beans	19.4	1 cup red lentils	6.4	¼ cup uncooked wheat berries	7.0
1 cup pinto beans	18.8	1 cup cooked whole wheat macaroni	5.7	¼ cup uncooked cracked wheat	6.0
1 cup blackberries, raw	8.8	1 cup whole wheat spinach noodles	6.0	2 ounces dry Vita Spelt	
3 tablespoons bran	6.0	½ cup oat bran	6.0	elbow macaroni	5.0
2 slices dark rye bread	5.8	½ cup green peas	9.1	1 Morningstar Farms Spicy	
2 slices whole wheat bread	6.0	½ cup black-eyed peas	8.0	Black Bean Burger	5.0
¾ cup broccoli, cooked	7.0	1 cup split peas	13.4	28g golden flaxseeds	6.0
1 cup cooked bulghur	9.6	1 medium russet potato	5.0	2 tablespoons brown flaxseeds	6.6
1 cup cooked carrots	8.8	1 medium sweet potato	6.8	¼ cup raw, hulled sunflower seeds	5.0
½ cup All-Bran or Bran Buds	10.4	½ cup raspberries	4.6	¼ cup unpopped popping corn	5.0
⅔ cup Bran Chex	5.0	1 cup cooked whole wheat spaghetti	5.6		
1 cup Bran Flakes	5.0	½ cup cooked spinach	7.0		

NOTE: measurements for beans, lentils, split peas, etc. are for cooked; fiber content is in grams.

people will warn you that there are indigestible carbohydrates and other compounds, particularly phytic acid and oxalic acid, in high-fiber foods that can actually reduce your intake of nutrients. However, this has been proven to be nothing to worry about. Studies comparing the availability of zinc in white and whole wheat bread, for instance, found that, though zinc was less available in the whole wheat bread, the net zinc absorption was greater with whole wheat than white simply because there was much more zinc present in the whole grain! Some of these acids are destroyed by fermentation, sprouting, and cooking, in any case. Fermentation of foods in the bowel (promoted by fiber) also helps the body absorb minerals.

When you begin to increase fiber in the diet, you may experience an increase in, well—flatulence. Don't despair! See page 107 for help. And be assured that, as your body gets used to more fiber, it will settle down!

What is soluble and insoluble fiber? Do I need both?

Soluble fiber gets its name from its ability to dissolve in water or other liquid. Soluble fibers include the pectin in fruits and the gums and mucilages of grains and legumes. These fibers bind with and eliminate excess cholesterol and toxins from the body. Soluble-fiber-rich foods include oats, oat bran, apples, peas, rice bran, citrus fruits, berries, dried beans, pearl barley, rye, potatoes, barley, raw cabbage, and flaxseeds.

Insoluble fiber (cellulose, lignin) does not dissolve in water, and is associated with decreasing the transit time of the stool in the colon, preventing constipation. Good sources include wheat bran, flaxseeds, whole wheat products, brown rice, mature vegetables, rye, and whole wheat pasta.

But the functions of these two types of fiber can overlap (soluble fiber also improves bowel movements, for instance), and most foods contain both types of fiber, though in varying amounts. The two types of fiber may have different jobs, but they are each equally important to our health, so we should eat a variety of unrefined foods daily in order to get enough of both.

INCREASING YOUR FIBER INTAKE NATURALLY

Let's look at a North American menu for one day, and see where we could add fiber. First, we'll look at a typical menu. I'm not going to make it horrendous—no terrible junk food—this person is obviously trying to eat well; then we'll take a look at a menu enhanced by fiber foods.

Nothing difficult to make—nothing weird! It's just a matter of making better choices with the knowledge you now have.

Breakfast
1 cup cornflakes—1 g fiber
1 cup milk—0 g
½ banana—1.5 g

Midmorning snack
2 rice cakes—0 g
2 tablespoons peanut butter—2 g
1 cup fruit juice—0 g

Lunch
Turkey sandwich with lettuce on light rye—2 g
1 cup vegetable soup—4 g
1 cup fruit yogurt—0 g

Afternoon snack
1 ounce baked tortilla chips—2 g
½ cup tomato salsa—1 g

Dinner
Baked chicken breast—0 g
½ cup green beans—2 g
Green salad with half a tomato—3 g
1 cup egg noodles—1 g
1 slice angel food cake

TOTAL GRAMS OF FIBER: 18.5

Let's see how we could do better:

Breakfast
1 cup bran flakes—5.0 g
1 cup milk or nondairy milk—0 g
½ cup blackberries—4.4 g

Midmorning snack
8 reduced-fat Triscuits—4 g
2 tablespoons peanut butter—2 g
1 cup fruit juice—0 g

Lunch
2 slices whole wheat bread—6 g
1 Morningstar Farms Spicy Black Bean Burger—5 g
1 cup vegetable soup—4 g
1 medium apple— 4 g

Afternoon snack
Popcorn (¼ cup dry popping corn)—5 g
2 carrots, cut into sticks—4 g

Dinner
1 cup Hormel Vegetarian Chili with Beans—7 g
2 corn muffins—2 g
Green salad with half a tomato—3 g
½ cup cooked spinach—7 g
Small piece of carrot cake—3 g

TOTAL GRAMS OF FIBER: 45.4

Tips for increasing your fiber intake

This book is chock full of delicious recipes to get you started on the road to a high-fiber diet, with information on cooking with beans and whole grains. But here are some simple and easy tips for increasing fiber:

1. Follow the new recommendations for eating 5-11 servings of fruits and vegetables a day.

2. Look at the Fiber Superstars list (page 17) and choose some foods from that list every day.

3. Eat beans! And lentils and dried peas. They are fiber powerhouses and protein-rich as well.

4. Go whole grain—not necessarily in everything, but for the majority of your meals.

5. Go for high-fiber cold cereals for breakfast.

6. Eat lots of berries. Add them to muffins, pancakes, even salads.

7. Eat brown rice instead of white whenever possible. Brown basmati is delicious.

8. Eat whole fruits instead of drinking juice.

9. Use flaxseeds as an egg replacer whenever possible. (See page 183). And add them to shakes and other foods.

10. Curb your intake of animal foods and go for a plant-based diet. Animal foods contain no fiber, so they crowd out fiber-rich foods.

11. Drink lots of water—9 glasses a day.

12. Eat soup! It can incorporate all sorts of high-fiber foods.

13. When filling your plate at mealtime, make sure half the plate is taken up by vegetables.

14. Don't be afraid of bread! Just make sure it's the whole grain variety.

15. Reduce fat and sweet foods in the diet. They can reduce your appetite for good plant foods.

16. Substitute whole wheat pastry flour for white flour in your home-baked goods.

17. Try different whole grain pastas—whole wheat, spelt, kamut, quinoa, brown rice.

18. Eat the skins of vegetables and fruits whenever possible.

19. Keep cleaned raw veggies in the fridge, along with a tasty dip for quick snacks.

20. Don't keep refined foods in the house. Stock up on whole grain crackers, baked corn tortilla chips, tomato salsa, nuts and dried fruits, popcorn, etc.

21. This book is filled with recipes and ideas to help you follow all of these suggestions. Use it.

FIBER AND CALORIE CONTENT OF SELECTED FOODS

FOOD	PORTION	CALORIES	FIBER(g)	FOOD	PORTION	CALORIES	FIBER(g)
Almonds, slivered	1 tbsp	14	0.6	Bran meal	3 tbsp	28	6.0
sliced	¼ cup	56	2.4		1 tbsp	9	2.0
Apple, raw	1 small	55-60*	3.0	Bran muffins (see Muffins)			
raw	1 med	70	4.0	Brazil nuts, shelled	2	48	2.5
raw	1 large	80-100*	4.5	Bread, Boston brown	2 slices	100	4.0*
baked	1 large	100	5.0	cracked wheat	2 slices	120	3.6
applesauce	⅔ cup	182	0.6	high-bran "health" bread	2 slices	120-160*	7.0*
Apricots, raw	1 whole	17	0.8	white	2 slices	160	1.9
dried	2 halves	36	1.7	dark rye (whole grain)	2 slices	108	5.8*
canned in syrup	3 halves	86	2.5	pumpernickel	2 slices	116	4.0
Artichokes, cooked	1 large	30-44*	4.5	seven-grain	2 slices	111-140	6.5
canned hearts	4-5 sm	24	4.5	whole wheat	2 slices	120	6.0
Asparagus, cooked,				whole wheat raisin	2 slices	140	6.5
small spears	½ cup	17	1.7	Bread crumbs, whole wheat	1 tbsp	22	2.5*
Avocado, diced	¼ cup	97	1.7	Broccoli, raw	½ cup	20	4.0
sliced	2 slices	50	0.9	frozen	4 spears	20	5.0
whole	½	170	2.8	fresh, cooked	¾ cup	30	7.0
Bacon-flavored				Brussel sprouts, cooked	¾ cup	36	3.0
chips (imitation)	1 tbsp	32	0.7*	Buckwheat groats (kasha)			
Baked beans in sauce				before cooking	½ cup	160	9.6*
(8-oz can)	1 cup	180*	16.0	cooked	1 cup	160	9.6
Baked potato (see Potatoes)				Bulghur, soaked, cooked	1 cup	160	9.6*
Banana	1 med 8"	96	3.0	Cabbage, white or red, raw	½ cup	8	1.5
Beans, black, cooked	1 cup	190	19.4	cooked	⅔ cup	15	3.0
broad beans (Italian, haricot)	¾ cup	30	3.0	Cantaloupe	¼	38	1.0*
Great Northern	1 cup	160	16.0	Carrots, raw, slivered (4-5 sticks)	¼ cup	10	1.7
kidney beans, canned	½ cup	94	9.7	cooked	½ cup	20	3.4
cooked	1 cup	188	19.4	Catsup (see Tomatoes)			
lima, Fordhook baby, butter	½ cup	118	3.7	Cauliflower, raw, chopped	3 tiny buds	10	1.2
lima, dried, canned or cooked	½ cup	150	5.8	cooked, chopped	⅞ cup	16	2.3
pinto, dried, before cooking	½ cup	155	18.8	Celery, Pascal, raw	¼ cup	5	2.0
canned or cooked	1 cup	155	18.8	chopped	2 tbsp	3	1.0
white, dried, before cooking	½ cup	160	16.0	cooked	½ cup	9	3.0
canned or cooked	½ cup	80	8.0	Cereal, All-Bran	3 tbsp	35	5.0
(See also Green beans, Chickpeas, Peas, Lentils)				(1½ oz)	½ cup	90	10.4
Bean sprouts, raw, in salad	¼ cup	7	0.8	Bran Buds	3 tbsp	35	5.0
Beet greens, cooked (see Greens)				(1½ oz)	½ cup	90	10.4
Beets, cooked, sliced	½ cup	33	2.5	Bran Chex	⅔ cup	90	5.0
whole	3 sm.	48	3.7*	Bran Flakes, plain	1 cup	90	5.0
Blackberries, raw, no sugar	½ cup	27	4.4	with raisins	1 cup	110	6.0
canned, in juice pack	½ cup	54	5.0	Cornflakes	3/4 cup	70	2.6
jam, with seeds	1 tbsp	60	0.7	Cracklin' Bran	1/2 cup	110	4.0

FOOD	PORTION	CALORIES	FIBER (g)
most cereals	1 cup	200	8.0
Oatmeal, dry	¾ cup	212	7.7
Nabisco 100% Bran	½ cup	105	4.0
Puffed wheat	1 cup	43	3.3
Raisin Bran	1 cup	195	5.0
Wheatena	⅔ cup	101	2.2
Wheaties	1 cup	104	2.0
Cherries, sweet, raw	10	28	1.2
	½ cup	55*	1.0*
Chestnuts, roasted	2 lg	29	1.9
Chickpeas (garbanzos) canned	½ cup	86	6.0
cooked	1 cup	172	12.0
Coconut, dried, sweetened	1 tbsp	46	3.4*
unsweetened	1 tbsp	22	3.4*
Corn (sweet), on cob	1 med ear	64-70*	5.0
kernels, cooked or canned	½ cup	64	5.0
cream-style, canned	½ cup	64	5.0
succotash (with limas)	½ cup	66	7.0
Cornbread (w/ regular cornmeal)	1 sq. (2½")	93	3.4
Crackers, cream	2	50	0.4
graham	2	53	1.4
Ry-Krisp	3	64	2.3
Triscuits	2	50	2.0
Wheat Thins	6	58	2.2
Cranberries, raw	¼ cup	12	2.0
sauce	½ cup	245	4.0
cranberry-orange relish	1 tbsp	56	0.5
Cucumber, raw, unpeeled	10 thin sl	12	0.7
Dates, pitted	2 (½ oz)	39	1.2*
Eggplant, baked with tomatoes	2 thick sl	42	4.0
Endive, raw salad	10 leaves	10	0.6
English muffins (see Muffins)			
Figs, dried	3	120	10.5
fresh	1	30	2.0
Fruit N' Fiber cereal	½ cup	90	3.5
Graham crackers (see Crackers)			
Grapefruit	½ (avg. size)	30	0.8
Grapes, white	20	75	1.0
red or black	15-20	65	1.0
Green (snap) beans, fresh/frozen	½ cup	10	2.1
Green peas (see Peas)			
Green peppers (see Peppers)			

FOOD	PORTION	CALORIES	FIBER (g)
Greens, cooked (collards, beet greens, dandelion, kale			
Swiss chard, turnip greens)	½ cup	20	4.0
Honeydew melon	3" slice	42	1.5
Kasha (see Buckwheat groats)			
Lasagne (see Macaroni)			
Lentils, brown, raw	⅓ cup	144	5.5
brown, cooked	⅔ cup	144	5.5
red, raw	½ cup	192	6.4
red, cooked	1 cup	192	6.4
Lettuce, (Boston, leaf, iceberg)	1 cup	5	0.8
Macaroni, whole wheat, cooked	1 cup	200	5.7
regular, frozen, baked, cheese	10 oz	506	2.2
Muffins, English, whole wheat	1 whole	125*	3.7
bran, whole wheat	2	136	4.6
Mushrooms, raw	5 sm	4	1.4
sauteed/baked w/ 2 tsp			
diet margarine	4 lg	45	2.0
canned sliced, water-pack	¼ cup	10	2.0
Noodles, whole wheat egg	1 cup	200	5.7
spinach whole wheat	1 cup	200	6.0
Okra fresh or frozen, cooked	½ cup	13	1.6
Olives, green	6	42	1.2
black	6-9	6	1.2
Onion, raw	1 tbsp	4	0.2
cooked	½ cup	22	1.5
instant minced	1 tbsp	6	0.3
green, raw (scallion)	¼ cup	11	0.8
Orange	1 lg	70	2.4
	1 sm	35	1.2
Parsley, chopped	2 tbsp	4	0.6
	1 tbsp	2	0.3
Parsnip, pared, cooked	1 lg	76	2.8
	1 sm	38	1.4
Peach, raw	1 med	38	2.3
canned in light syrup	2 halves	70	1.4
Peanut butter	1 tbsp	86	1.1
homemade	1 tbsp	70	1.5
Peanuts, dry roasted	1 tbsp	52	1.1
Pear	1 med	88	4.0
Peas, green, fresh or frozen	½ cup	60	9.1
black-eyed frozen/canned	½ cup	74	8.0
split, cooked (See Chickpeas)	1 cup	126	13.4

FOOD	PORTION	CALORIES	FIBER (g)	FOOD	PORTION	CALORIES	FIBER (g)
Peas and carrots frozen (5oz)	½ package	40	6.2	Split peas (see Peas)			
Peppers, green sweet, raw	2 tbsp	4	0.3	Squash, summer (yellow)	½ cup	8	2.0
green sweet, cooked	½ cup	13	1.2	winter, baked or mashed	½ cup	40-50	3.5
red sweet (pimento)	2 tbsp	9	1.0	zucchini, raw or cooked	½ cup	7	3.0
red chili, fresh	1 tbsp	7	1.2	Strawberries, without sugar	1 cup	45	3.0
dried, crushed	1 tsp	7	1.2	Succotash (see Corn)			
Pimento (see Peppers)				Sunflower kernels	1 tbsp	65	0.5*
Pineapple, fresh, cubed	½ cup	41	0.8	Sweet potatoes (see Potatoes)			
canned	1 cup	58-74*	0.8	Swiss chard (see Greens)			
Plums	2 or 3 sm	38-45*	2.0	Tomatoes, raw	1 sm.	22	1.4
Popcorn (unbuttered)	1 cup	20	1.0	canned	½ cup	21	1.0
Potatoes, Idaho, baked	1 sm (6 oz)	120	4.2	sauce	½ cup	20	0.5
(7 oz)	1 med	140	5.0	catsup	1 tbsp	18	0.2
all-purpose white/russet	1 sm	60	2.2	Tortillas	2	140	4.0*
boiled (5 oz)	1 med	100	3.5	Turnip, white raw, slivered	¼ cup	8	1.2
mashed (w/ 1 tbsp milk)	½ cup	85	3.0	cooked	½ cup	16	2.0
sweet, baked or boiled	1 sm (5 oz)	146	4.0	Walnuts, English, shelled, chopped	1 tbsp	49	1.1
(See also Yams)				Watercress, raw (20 sprigs)	½ cup	4	1.0
Prunes, pitted	3	122	1.9	Watermelon	1 thick slice	68	2.8
Radishes	3	5	0.1	Wheat Thins (see Crackers)			
Raisins	1 tbsp	29	1.0	Yams, cooked or baked in skin	1 med (6oz)	156	6.8
Raspberries, red, fresh/frozen	½ cup	20	4.6	Zucchini (see Squash)			
Raspberry jam	1 tbsp	75	1.0				
Rhubarb, cooked with sugar	½ cup	169*	2.9				
Rice, white (before cooking)	½ cup	79	2.0				
brown (before cooking)	½ cup	83	5.5				
instant	1 serv	79	0.7				
Rutabaga (yellow turnip)	½ cup	40	3.2				
Sauerkraut, canned	⅔ cup	15	3.1				
Scallion (see Onion)							
Shredded wheat, large biscuit	1 piece	74	2.2				
spoon size	1 cup	168	4.4				
Spaghetti, whole wheat, plain	1 cup	200	5.6				
with tomato sauce	1 cup	220	6.0				
Spinach, raw	1 cup	8	3.5				
cooked	½ cup	26	7.0				

*Important as dietary fiber is, laboratory technicians have not yet been able to ascertain the exact total content in many foods, especially vegetables and fruits, because of its complexity. Consequently, estimates vary from one source to another. Where differing estimates have been found, an approximation is given in the chart, as indicated by an asterisk. The same symbol following calorie content means the number of calories has been estimated, varying according to other added ingredients, especially fats and sugars, and to the size of the "average" fruit or vegetable unit.

FROM:
www.bethisraelny.org/healthinfo/dietaryfiber/fibercontentchart.html

BREAKFAST

Breakfast is an excellent meal for introducing fiber-rich foods into your diet, and is perhaps the meal most in need of revamping in North America. Millions of North Americans eat no breakfast at all, falling prey later in the morning to the temptations of doughnut shops and candy bars, or swilling sugary coffee and cola drinks in a vain attempt to fend off the fatigue and crankiness that signals low blood sugar. Many others start the day with fatty repasts of fried eggs, bacon, fried ham and/or sausages (often accompanied by fried potatoes, buttered white toast, or white-flour pancakes dripping butter and artificial syrup), which cause sluggishness as well as clogging the arteries. Even without all of the sugar and fat, the refined-flour products, stripped of their fiber (never mind all the nutrients that are left behind!), are rapidly absorbed by the body, just like sugars, leaving you feeling weak and hungry a mere hour or two later.

Having fiber in the digestive tract helps slow the speed at which all sugar—including natural sugar—is absorbed. The energy, or calories, from high-fiber foods are still being absorbed after the sugar is digested, preventing that low blood sugar slump. Scientists are optimistic that studies now in progress will show that eating a high-fiber diet could actually reduce the amount of insulin that diabetics require, and perhaps prevent adult-onset, or Type II, diabetes. But, even if you do not have diabetes, the effect of a high-fiber breakfast can help you to have a more productive morning.

A light breakfast containing fruit, whole grains in any form, and a little bit of protein is easily digested and contains enough protein, fiber, and complex carbohydrates to keep you alert, energetic, and productive until your lunch break. This type of breakfast can be as simple as a fruit smoothie or fresh fruit and (soy) yogurt with whole grain toast, or a bowl of commercial whole grain cereal and nondairy milk with fruit, but you may require a more substantial meal. It does not have to be loaded with refined carbohydrates and saturated fat in order to be hearty. Try some of the low-fat, high-fiber pancake and waffle recipes in this chapter, and accompany them with some of the delicious and low-fat meatless "sausages" and "bacon" that are now widely available in supermarkets and health food stores throughout North America.

(See the Bread chapter, pages 36-53, for additional breakfast ideas.)

BIRCHER MUESLI

Makes 4 servings

Bircher Muesli was invented by a Dr. Bircher-Benner in Switzerland in the late 1800s as a nutritious, raw, but digestible breakfast cereal. You can buy expensive commercial versions, but the original is cheap and very easy to make, as long as you start it the night before.

THE NIGHT BEFORE: Soak the oats and milk in a bowl overnight in the refrigerator. Add the remaining ingredients just before serving. Serve with nondairy milk, soy yogurt, maple syrup or sugar, and more fresh fruit (such as berries), if desired.

1½ cups rolled oats
(or other whole grain rolled cereal)

1½ cups nondairy milk

2 tablespoons wheat bran
or raw wheat germ

2 tablespoons currants, raisins,
or other dried fruit

¼ teaspoon salt

¼-½ cup chopped toasted almonds,
filberts (hazelnuts), or sunflower seeds

2 small shredded unpeeled apples

3 tablespoons lemon juice

Maple syrup to taste

Single Serving

6 tablespoons oatmeal

6 tablespoons nondairy milk

1 teaspoon bran or wheat germ

1 teaspoon dried fruit

pinch of salt

1 tablespoon chopped nuts

½ small apple, shredded

2¼ teaspoons lemon juice

PER SERVING:			
Calories	277	FIBER	8.6g
Total Fat	10g	Carbohydrate	41g
Saturated Fat	1g	Protein	10g
Calories from fat	32%	Sodium	148mg

MICROWAVE MAPLE COCONUT GRANOLA

Makes 3¼ cups

It's difficult to make fat-free granola in the oven, because it dries out. The microwave works perfectly for this, and it's possible to make small batches. (This recipe is for a large microwave.) I avoided granola for years because of the high fat content, until I devised this easy recipe. It's far cheaper and more nutritious than commercial low-fat varieties.

2 cups rolled oats or other whole grain rolled cereal

¾ cup whole wheat or other whole grain flour OR ½ cup flour plus ¼ cup wheat germ

½ cup wheat, oat, or rice bran

⅓ cup maple syrup

¼-½ teaspoon cinnamon

¼ teaspoon salt

¼ teaspoon coconut extract

OPTIONAL

½ cup dried fruit

½ cup chopped nuts, seeds, or unsweetened shredded coconut, or a mixture

Mix well with hands. (Do not add optional dried fruit until after cooking.) Spread evenly on waxed paper on the microwave. Cook on HIGH for 3 minutes. Stir and spread evenly again. Cook on HIGH 3 minutes more. Let stand 3 minutes. Add the optional dried fruit, if you like. When completely cool, store in an airtight container.

TIP: Without the dried fruit, this makes a good nut substitute for low-fat baking.

Orange-Nut Granola

Add the following ingredients to the oats, flour, and bran.

3 tablespoons unsweetened shredded coconut

⅓ cup chopped nuts

¼ cup frozen orange juice concentrate

2 tablespoons maple syrup

½ teaspoon orange extract

½ teaspoon cinnamon

¼ teaspoon salt

¼ teaspoon coconut extract

PER SERVING: ½ cup			
Calories	208	FIBER	6.7g
Total Fat	2g	Carbohydrate	43g
Saturated Fat	0g	Protein	7g
Calories from fat	8%	Sodium	92mg

Brown Rice & Spice Breakfast Cereal

Makes 4-6 servings

Mix all of the ingredients in a heavy-bottomed medium saucepan. Stir over medium heat until bubbly, then simmer on low heat, stirring often, 5-10 minutes, or until the rice has absorbed most of the milk.

MICROWAVE OPTION: Mix all of the ingredients in a microwave-safe bowl, cover with a plate, and cook on HIGH 3-5 minutes, or until most of the milk is absorbed and mixture is hot. Serve hot with more nondairy milk.

3 cups leftover cooked brown rice

Nondairy milk to cover the rice

¼ cup maple syrup

½ cup raisins, currants, or other dried fruit

½ teaspoon cinnamon

¼ teaspoon freshly grated nutmeg

1 tablespoon grated orange rind (optional)

PER SERVING:			
Calories	227	FIBER	3.6g
Total Fat	2g	Carbohydrate	50g
Saturated Fat	0g	Protein	4g
Calories from fat	7%	Sodium	16mg

3 Bears' Porridge

Makes 2 servings

To avoid the overnight soak in this recipe, use a fine bulghur.

THE NIGHT BEFORE: Mix all of the ingredients in a heavy medium saucepan or a 1 quart microwave-safe bowl. Cover and let stand until morning.

IN THE MORNING: Bring the mixture to a boil over medium-high heat, then cook over medium heat until thickened, about 8 minutes, or microwave on HIGH, covered, 5-7 minutes. Serve hot with your favorite nondairy milk and your favorite sweetener.

1½ cups water

½ cup bulghur wheat

3 tablespoons rolled oats (or other whole grain rolled cereal)

¼ cup raisins, currants, dates, or other chopped dried fruit (or a mixture)

Pinch each of salt and cinnamon

TIP: For 1 serving, reduce all ingredients by half and cook 4 minutes in the microwave.

PER SERVING:			
Calories	181	FIBER	7.4g
Total Fat	1g	Carbohydrate	41g
Saturated Fat	0g	Protein	5g
Calories from fat	4%	Sodium	22mg

FRUITY OATMEAL

Makes 1 serving

This is my breakfast four or five days a week. It's cheap, filling, nutritious, high-fiber, comforting, and, oh, yes!—delicious, too! Forget flavored oatmeal in a packet—this is easy to make, especially in the microwave. For the apple, you can substitute other fruit in season— peaches, pears, and apricots are delectable!

¾ cup water

½ medium apple, cored, but not peeled, and chopped

⅓ cup rolled oats (or other rolled whole grain)

1 tablespoon wheat bran (or rice bran)

½ tablespoon ground flaxseeds

Pinch of salt

Pinch of cinnamon (optional)

Mix all of the ingredients in a small heavy saucepan and bring to a boil. Reduce the heat to medium-low and cook, stirring occasionally, 5 minutes. Cover and remove from heat. Let stand 2 or 3 minutes before serving.

MICROWAVE OPTION: Combine all of the ingredients in a microwave-safe bowl large enough to accommodate boiling-up. Cook on HIGH, uncovered, 4 minutes.

Serve hot with maple syrup or brown sugar and your favorite nondairy milk.

NOTE: This is chewy oatmeal. If you like the creamy kind, increase the water to 1 cup, and cook it 8 minutes.

TIP: Don't leave out the salt. Oatmeal tastes flat without it.

PER SERVING:			
Calories	166	FIBER	6.9g
Total Fat	3g	Carbohydrate	32g
Saturated Fat	0g	Protein	6g
Calories from fat	16%	Sodium	23mg

CRISPY WHOLE GRAIN WAFFLES

Makes about ten 4-inch waffles

You can make whole grain waffles from an ordinary waffle recipe—but why spoil a good thing with all those eggs and melted butter? Try these crispy, ultra-nutritious homemade waffles. Don't be put off by having to put the soybeans (or other beans) on to soak the night before. This takes just minutes before you retire for the night, and then, in the morning, the batter is quickly made in the blender while the waffle iron heats up. These waffles are inexpensive and low in fat, but contain high-quality protein, fiber, and other nutrients— a great way to start the day! They can also be used as a lunch or supper dish, topped with chili or creamed vegetables, etc. Keep some ready-made in the freezer for quick toaster snacks—they are great eaten out of hand with a little low-sugar (ultra-lite) jam. My favorite version is made with soybeans and half whole wheat flour, half stone-ground cornmeal. And, don't worry, no one will suspect that there are beans in these waffles!

½ cup dried soybeans or chickpeas

2¼ cups water (Substitute fruit juice for some of the water, if you wish.)

1½ cups rolled oats OR 1¼ cups whole wheat flour, brown rice flour, or stone-ground cornmeal or a mixture

¼ cup wheat or rice bran

2 tablespoons sugar, maple syrup, or other sweetener

3 tablespoons flaxseeds

1 tablespoon baking powder

1 teaspoon salt

OPTIONAL

½ tablespoon vanilla, lemon, or orange extract

Pinch of citrus zest

½ cup finely chopped toasted nuts or unsweetened shredded coconut

THE NIGHT BEFORE: Soak the soybeans or chickpeas in plenty of water. (If you aren't sure when you'll be making the waffles, feel free to safely leave the beans in water in the refrigerator for up to a week.)

IN THE MORNING: Drain the beans. Blend the beans and all of the remaining ingredients in a blender until smooth, light, and foamy. This may take several minutes. Let the batter stand while you heat the waffle iron.

Even if you have a nonstick waffle iron, spray the grids well with oil or nonstick cooking spray. If you have an older iron, you may have to grease it with vegetable shortening to keep the waffles from sticking. (You can sometimes find a nonhydrogenated version at health food stores.) If using that much fat is a problem, then you should probably get a newer, nonstick waffle iron—there are some very inexpensive models.

When the iron is hot, pour on a heaping ⅓ cup batter for each 4-inch square waffle. Close the iron and set the timer for 8 minutes. Don't check before 8 minutes is up. If the iron is hard to open, cook a couple of minutes more. The waffle should be golden-brown and crispy. Serve immediately, or let cool on cake racks.

Spray the iron with oil or nonstick cooking spray before you make each batch of waffles. Blend the batter again briefly before pouring out each waffle. If the batter gets thicker on standing, add a little water to reach the right consistency.

These waffles take a little longer to bake than ordinary waffles (about 8 minutes), so you might want to make them ahead of time, or have two waffle irons going at the same time. They can be reheated quickly in a very hot oven for a short time (you just want to crisp and heat them, not dry them out), or in a toaster.

TIP: Refrigerate leftover batter in the blender with the lid on. You can re-blend the batter—adding a tiny bit more water if the batter has become too thick—just before cooking the waffles.

When waffles are cool, they can be frozen in plastic bags or rigid containers. Thaw and serve with your favorite toppings.

NOTE: Do not try to use spelt flour or spelt. Spelt makes a very heavy waffle.

VARIATION #1: Instead of using flour, meal, or rolled oats, soak 1 cup wheat kernels (wheat berries) from soft or hard wheat or brown rice in the 2¼ cups water overnight. Do not drain; add grain and water to the drained beans and remaining ingredients, and proceed with recipe.

VARIATION #2: If you forgot to soak beans or decided to make waffles on the spur of the moment, try this: Instead of using beans, substitute ⅓ cup chopped nuts or seeds or ¼ cup nut butter. You can use raw or roasted nuts, seeds, or nut butters. You can use cashews, almonds, pecans, filberts or hazelnuts, walnuts, Brazil nuts, sunflower seeds, sesame seeds, etc.—even peanuts. Mix and cook just as for the basic recipe.

PER SERVING: each

Calories	111	FIBER	3.8g
Total Fat	4g	Carbohydrate	15g
Saturated Fat	1g	Protein	6g
Calories from fat	32%	Sodium	323mg

Featherlight Cornmeal-Orange-Pecan Pancakes

Makes about 24 four-inch pancakes

Fruit juice and whole wheat pastry flour make an extra-light eggless pancake that is as good-for-you as it is delicious.

In a large bowl, whisk together the flour, cornmeal, soy or chickpea flour, baking powder, baking soda, and salt. Add all of the remaining ingredients and stir just until mixed. Lumps are okay. (This batter is a little runnier than ordinary pancake batter.)

Heat a nonstick griddle or skillet or a heavy cast-iron griddle or skillet over high heat until drops of water dance on the surface. Reduce heat to medium; if using an electric griddle, reduce the heat to 325°F. Rub a little oil over the surface with a scrunched-up paper towel. Spoon the batter onto the griddle, using a scant ¼ cup per pancake. They spread a little, so don't crowd them.

When bubbles appear on the tops, loosen pancakes carefully with a pancake turner and flip them gently.

When the underside is golden and the inside is cooked (you can check one with

1½ cups whole wheat pastry flour OR
1¼ cups whole wheat flour

1 cup stone-ground cornmeal

¼ cup soy flour or chickpea flour

1 teaspoon baking powder

1 teaspoon baking soda

1 teaspoon salt

2 cups orange juice
(freshly squeezed, preferably)

1 cup water

2 tablespoons finely grated
(organic) orange zest

1 tablespoon oil

½ cup finely chopped toasted pecans
or unsweetened shredded coconut

a fork to make sure), serve immediately. Do not overcook. The pancakes should still be a bit puffy when you take them off the griddle. If they are overcooked, they won't be as light and cakey as they should be. Serve hot with maple syrup or your other favorite toppings.

NOTE: For more fiber, add 2 tablespoons ground flaxseeds. They won't be quite as "featherlight," however.

PER SERVING: each			
Calories	83	FIBER	1.8g
Total Fat	3g	Carbohydrate	12g
Saturated Fat	0g	Protein	2g
Calories from fat	32%	Sodium	158mg

OATMEAL-APPLE-WALNUT PANCAKES

Makes about 24 four-inch pancakes

Serve these hot with maple syrup or your other favorite toppings.

In a large bowl, whisk together the wheat flour, oat flour, soy or chickpea flour, baking powder, baking soda, and salt. Add all of the remaining ingredients and stir just until mixed. Lumps are okay. (This is a little runnier than ordinary pancake batter.)

Heat a nonstick griddle or skillet or a heavy cast-iron griddle or skillet over high heat until drops of water dance on the surface. Reduce heat to medium; if using an electric griddle, reduce the heat to 325°F. Rub a little oil over the surface with a scrunched-up paper towel. Spoon the batter onto the griddle, using a scant ¼ cup per pancake. They spread a little, so don't crowd them.

When bubbles appear on the tops, loosen pancakes carefully with a pancake turner and flip them gently.

When the underside is golden and the inside is cooked (you can check one with a fork to make sure), serve immediately. Do not overcook. The pancakes should still be a bit puffy when you take them off the griddle. If they are overcooked, won't be as light and cakey as they should be.

2 cups whole wheat pastry flour

½ cup oat flour (rolled oats ground fine in a DRY blender)

¼ cup soy flour or chickpea flour

1 teaspoon baking soda

1 teaspoon baking powder

1 teaspoon salt

Freshly grated nutmeg to taste

Large pinch of cinnamon

2 cups unsweetened apple juice

1 cup water

1 tablespoon oil

1 teaspoon vanilla

½ cup finely chopped toasted walnuts or pecans

1 medium unpeeled apple, cored and finely chopped

NOTE: For more fiber, add 2 tablespoons ground flaxseeds. They won't be quite as light, however.

TIP: To use this as a basic pancake recipe, use 2½ cups whole wheat pastry flour, or the same combo of flour and oats, but omit the spices, vanilla, nuts, and apple.

PER SERVING: each			
Calories	87	FIBER	2g
Total Fat	3g	Carbohydrate	13g
Saturated Fat	0g	Protein	3g
Calories from fat	31%	Sodium	157mg

Eggless Crêpes

Makes 12-13 crêpes

These are excellent—they have that flexible, texture of traditional crêpes. They freeze well, too.

Process all ingredients in a food processor or blender until very smooth. Heat a nonstick 8-inch skillet over medium-high heat and wipe it lightly with oil before making each crêpe. Stir the batter before you make each crêpe. Use about 3 tablespoons of batter per crêpe, tilting the pan until the batter covers the pan evenly. Cook for a few seconds, or until the top looks dry. Carefully loosen the crêpe with a spatula and flip. After a few seconds, the other side should be dry. Remove from the pan and fold into quarters or roll like a jelly roll and place on a plate (or leave them flat if you are going to stack them with filling).

Fill the crêpes and serve; or cover with a clean tea towel, cool, and place in a plastic bag or rigid container (with pieces of waxed paper between each crêpe) and refrigerate for up to 3 days; or freeze them for future use (thaw thoroughly before filling).

1½ cups soymilk

1 cup whole wheat pastry flour

½ cup medium-firm tofu

¼ cup soy flour

1 tablespoon sugar

½ teaspoon salt

½ teaspoon baking powder

¼ teaspoon turmeric

Freshly grated nutmeg to taste

1-2 tablespoons nutritional yeast flakes (Optional)

DESSERT CRÊPES: Use 2 tablespoons sugar, and add 1 teaspoon vanilla and ½ teaspoon orange or lemon extract to basic recipe. Fill with nondairy cream cheese, and top with sweetened fresh fruit, liqueur, and/or any sweet sauce.

SAFFRON CRÊPES: Add ¼ teaspoon Spanish saffron to basic recipe.

BUCKWHEAT CRÊPES: Substitute ½ cup buckwheat flour for ½ cup of the wheat flour in the basic recipe, and use soured soymilk (add about 1 tablespoon lemon juice to the soymilk) or ¾ cup soy yogurt plus ¾ cup soymilk.

PER SERVING:

Calories	60	FIBER	2.1g
Total Fat	2g	Carbohydrate	9g
Saturated Fat	0g	Protein	4g
Calories from fat	30%	Sodium	5mg

Blender Fruit Smoothie

Makes 1 serving

Blend all of the ingredients in a blender until very smooth. Serve immediately.

¾ cup orange juice or other fruit juice or soy yogurt

1 heaping tablespoon isolated soy protein powder OR
2 tablespoons raw cashew pieces

1 tablespoon flaxseeds

½ frozen banana (peeled before freezing), cut into chunks

1 small handful berries or chunks of mango, peach, or other fresh or frozen fruit

OPTIONAL

Sweetener of choice to taste (This can be a low-sugar jam if you have no fruit other than bananas around.)

¼ teaspoon dairy-free acidophilus powder

¼ teaspoon coconut, almond, or vanilla extract

PER SERVING:			
Calories	173	FIBER	4.7g
Total Fat	6g	Carbohydrate	22g
Saturated Fat	1g	Protein	10g
Calories from fat	31%	Sodium	40mg

PIÑA COLADA SMOOTHIE: Use pineapple juice instead of orange juice, pineapple chunks instead of berries or other fruit, and add ¼ teaspoon coconut extract and a few drops of rum extract (optional).

Strawberry-Almond Smoothie

Makes 2 servings

Strawberries and flaxseeds make this beverage high-fiber! Use frozen berries to make a frothy, cold shake.

Blend all of the ingredients in a blender until very smooth. Serve immediately.

10 medium frozen strawberries (5 large), chopped

1 cup nondairy milk

½ cup firm SILKEN tofu OR
¼ cup raw cashew pieces plus ¼ cup nondairy milk

2 tablespoons sugar OR Grade A light maple syrup

1 tablespoon flaxseeds

¼-½ teaspoon pure almond extract

PER SERVING:			
Calories	198	FIBER	5.8g
Total Fat	4g	Carbohydrate	40g
Saturated Fat	0g	Protein	4g
Calories from fat	18%	Sodium	3mg

BREADS

Bread is a common and well-loved food that has the potential to be health-giving and nutritious, yet the majority of bread is made of flour that's been stripped of its nutrition and fiber. White flour may produce fluffy, light products, but we pay big bucks for white bread when we could make it ourselves not only much more cheaply, but also much more nutritiously, with high-fiber whole grains.

Eating whole grain bread is a simple way to add fiber to your diet. And making bread is not difficult. Yes, it takes a while to rise, but that is a time when you could go about your other tasks. And nothing impresses company as much as delicious, homemade, whole grain bread.

See more about whole grain and low-fat baking in the Desserts chapter, and more about whole grain flours on the next page.

TYPES OF WHOLE WHEAT FLOURS

◆ *Graham flour* is whole wheat flour that is a little coarser and has added bran.

◆ *Whole wheat flour,* like white all-purpose flour, has less gluten than bread flour, but more than pastry flour. Most supermarkets carry this type of flour.

◆ *Whole wheat bread flour*, *hard-wheat flour,* or *high-gluten flour* is made from hard wheat and has a higher level of protein and gluten than all-purpose flour or cake and pastry flour. Protein and gluten are necessary for bread to allow the structure that causes rising and gives bread texture.

◆ *Whole wheat pastry flour* is made from soft wheat, which has less protein (gluten) than hard wheat flour. This delicate flour is excellent for lightly textured whole grain muffins and other quick breads, and cakes and pastries. Don't use it for making yeast breads, however, because it doesn't contain enough gluten to make satisfactory yeast breads. Use this type of flour for low-fat (unyeasted) baked goods. Because fat coats the gluten in flour, making it tender, use all-purpose flour in recipes containing sufficient fat. In fat-free or very low-fat recipes (including those that use applesauce or other fat substitutes), pastry flour will result in a more delicate product.

◆ *Wheat bran or bran* is the outer coating of the wheat kernel, which is removed to make white flour. It is high in fiber. You can boost fiber in many baked goods by adding a little bran.

◆ *Wheat germ* is another nutritious part of the wheat kernel removed during the making of white flour. It contains some fiber and many nutrients. Wheat germ contains some fat so it is best kept in the freezer to prevent rancidity. The toasted variety is sold in jars in most supermarkets. Raw wheat germ is available in natural food stores and some supermarkets.

◆ *White whole wheat flour* is a fairly new product on the market. It is milled from white winter wheat and has a lighter color and milder, sweeter flavor than regular whole wheat flour, but is identical nutritionally.

◆ *Whole durum wheat flour* is milled from very high-protein wheat, and is excellent for making extruded pastas. Be sure the whole wheat pasta you purchase is made from this flour. It's mild in flavor and has a pale golden color.

QUICKBREADS

Quickbreads are so-named because they are quick and easy to make—perfect for last-minute meals. Mix quickbreads and muffins briefly and gently so that they stay tender and light.

BEER BREAD

Makes 1 large or 2 small loaves, 16 servings

Beer gives this easy fat-free bread a yeasty aroma and flavor, and a chewy crust.

Preheat the oven to 350°F. Lightly oil one 4 x 8-inch loaf pan or two 3 x 6-inch loaf pans.

In a medium bowl, combine all of the ingredients except the beer. Add the beer and stir briefly, just until moistened. Spoon dough into prepared pans. Bake 35-45 minutes until cake tester inserted in center comes out clean. Remove from pans. Cover with a towel and cool on a rack.

2¼ cups whole wheat flour

3 tablespoons sugar

1 tablespoon baking powder

1 teaspoon salt

½ teaspoon baking soda

1 (12-ounce) can of beer, ale, or stout (can be nonalcoholic), at room temperature

OPTIONAL

2 teaspoons dried dill weed (or 2 tablespoons fresh) PLUS 1 tablespoon dehydrated onion flakes (or ¼ cup minced fresh onion) OR 1 teaspoon caraway seeds OR ½ cup minced fresh herbs

PER SERVING:			
Calories	122	FIBER	2.7g
Total Fat	0g	Carbohydrate	25g
Saturated Fat	0g	Protein	4g
Calories from fat	0%	Sodium	298mg

Perfect Cornbread

Makes 8-12 servings

This is my favorite cornbread—Yankee-style, since it's a little sweet. It's moist and corny, high-fiber and low in fat.

Oil a 10-inch cast-iron skillet and place it in the oven as it preheats to 375°F. Whisk all of the dry ingredients together in a medium bowl. In a separate bowl, whisk together the wet ingredients. Add the wet ingredients to the dry ingredients; mix briefly (do not beat) and pour into hot skillet. Bake 20 minutes.

NOTE: For Southern-style cornbread, use white stone-ground cornmeal and omit sugar or use only 1 tablespoon.

CORN MUFFINS: Bake the batter in 12 oiled muffin cups 25 minutes at 400°F. You can add ⅔ cup chopped toasted walnuts or pecans and/or 1 cup fresh cranberries or blueberries (½ cup dried) or ¾ cup chopped pitted prunes.

HOT CHILE SURPRISE CORN MUFFINS: Make muffins as directed above. Fill half of each muffin cup with batter. Spoon about 2 teaspoons of hot red pepper or jalapeño jelly onto the batter. Top with the remaining batter and bake as above.

DRY MIXTURE

1 cup stone-ground cornmeal

¾ cup whole wheat pastry flour

⅓ cup soy or chickpea flour

¼ cup sugar

1 teaspoon baking powder

¾ teaspoon salt

½ teaspoon baking soda

WET MIXTURE

1¼ cup nondairy milk with 1 tablespoon lemon juice added

¼ cup smooth unsweetened applesauce

2 tablespoons oil or melted nondairy margarine

PER SERVING:			
Calories	143	FIBER	3g
Total Fat	5g	Carbohydrate	23g
Saturated Fat	0g	Protein	4g
Calories from fat	31%	Sodium	268mg

GREEN CHILE CORNBREAD OR CORN MUFFINS: Add 1 (4-ounce) can green chilies, drained well, to the batter. Before baking, sprinkle the top of each muffin with ½-1 tablespoon nondairy Parmesan cheese.

Oatmeal Drop Scones or Biscuits

Makes 12 biscuits

Old traditional Scottish scone recipes contained no fat at all. They were eaten immediately, warm and fresh, as these should be.

Preheat oven to 400°F. Oil a cookie sheet.

Combine oat flour, flour, sugar, soda, and salt in a medium bowl; mix well.

In a separate, smaller bowl, mix the milk and lemon juice. Pour into the dry ingredients and mix briefly with a fork. Drop by large spoonfuls onto prepared pan. Smooth tops a bit. Sprinkle with optional topping of choice, if using. Bake 15 minutes. Split with a fork.

CURRANT SCONES: Add ¼-½ cup dried currants, ¾ cup grated apple (optional) and 3 tablespoons sugar (optional). Omit ¼ cup of the milk if you add the apple.

HERB SCONES: Add ½ cup loosely packed chopped fresh herbs of choice.

1 cup rolled oats, ground in a dry blender to a fine meal

1¼ cups whole wheat pastry flour or unbleached white flour

1 teaspoon sugar

½ teaspoon baking soda

½ teaspoon salt

1¼ cups nondairy milk

1 tablespoon lemon juice or vinegar

OPTIONAL TRADITIONAL TOPPINGS
Sugar

Caraway seeds

PER SERVING:			
Calories	86	FIBER	2.7g
Total Fat	1g	Carbohydrate	15g
Saturated Fat	0g	Protein	4g
Calories from fat	10%	Sodium	144mg

Tender No-Fat
BANANA BREAD

Makes one 9 x 5-inch loaf or 16 servings

The tofu and banana make this bread moist and tender. Note: For a very tender bread, stir the batter as little as possible.

Preheat oven to 350°F. Oil a 9 x 5-inch loaf pan.

Blend the wet ingredients in a blender. In a medium bowl, mix the dry ingredients. Stir in the blended mixture and mix only briefly. Add dates and nuts if desired, stirring briefly. Pour into prepared pan. Bake 1 hour. Cool a few minutes, then turn out on rack to cool.

WET MIXTURE

8 ounces medium-firm regular tofu OR
1 cup firm or extra-firm SILKEN tofu

¼ cup water or juice

¾ cup sugar or Sucanat

2 medium ripe bananas, peeled and chunked

2 teaspoons vanilla

Zest of 1 orange

DRY MIXTURE

2 cups whole wheat pastry flour

2 teaspoons baking powder

½ teaspoon salt

½ teaspoon baking soda

½ teaspoon freshly grated nutmeg (optional)

¾ cup chopped pitted dates or other dried fruit

½ cup chopped nuts (optional)

PER SERVING:			
Calories	142	FIBER	3.1g
Total Fat	1g	Carbohydrate	30g
Saturated Fat	0g	Protein	4g
Calories from fat	6%	Sodium	113mg

Old-Fashioned
BRAN BREAD

Makes one 9 x 5-inch loaf, 16 slices

We tend to think that all old-fashioned breads were full of eggs, cream, and butter, but that's not so! Try this delicious example of old-time low-fat baking.

Preheat the oven to 350°F. Oil a 9 x 5-inch loaf pan.

Mix the wet ingredients in the blender. Mix the dry ingredients in a medium bowl. Stir in the raisins and nuts. Pour in the wet ingredients and stir just until mixed. Do not beat. Pour into prepared pan and bake 1 hour. Let cool in the pan on a rack for 15 minutes, then loosen carefully and remove from pan. Cool completely on rack before slicing.

WET MIXTURE
1 cup brown sugar

2 tablespoons lemon juice
with nondairy milk to make 2 cups

DRY MIXTURE
2 cups wheat bran

2 cups whole wheat or unbleached flour

2 teaspoons baking soda

1 teaspoon salt

1 cup raisins or other dried fruit

½ cup chopped nuts

PER SERVING:

Calories	231	FIBER	7.6g
Total Fat	5g	Carbohydrate	46g
Saturated Fat	0g	Protein	6g
Calories from fat	19%	Sodium	372mg

IRISH SODA BREAD

Makes 1 large or 2 small loaves, 20 slices

Called "soda bread" in Ireland and "bannock" in Scotland and parts of Canada, this simple quick bread is tender and delicious.

Preheat the oven to 450°F. In a medium bowl, mix the dry ingredients, including any optionals. Stir in the milk mixture and mix briefly. Knead 30 seconds. Pat into 1 large or 2 smaller rounds about 1½ inches thick. Place on a nonstick or lightly oiled and floured baking sheet or 2 round cake pans. Slash a ¼-inch-deep cross in the top of each loaf with a sharp knife or razor blade.

Bake 10 minutes; reduce the heat to 375°F and bake 30 minutes more or until crusty. Serve hot or cover with a tea towel and cool on a rack.

FOR A RICHER VERSION: With your fingers, cut 2-4 tablespoons very cold nondairy margarine or nonhydrogenated shortening into the dry ingredients until crumbly.

4 cups whole wheat pastry flour OR
1 cup oat flour* and 3 cups whole wheat pastry flour

1 to 4 tablespoons sugar or Sucanat

1½ teaspoons salt

1 teaspoon baking soda

1⅞ cups nondairy milk
with 2 tablespoons lemon juice or vinegar added

OPTIONAL

1 cup dried currants or raisins

½ teaspoon freshly ground nutmeg

*Oat flour: grind rolled oats in a DRY blender.

PER SERVING:			
Calories	122	FIBER	3.9g
Total Fat	1g	Carbohydrate	22g
Saturated Fat	0g	Protein	5g
Calories from fat	7%	Sodium	250mg

Frankly Fibrous
CHOCOLATE CHIP BRAN MUFFINS

Makes 12 muffins

If you claim not to like bran muffins, try these. They are very branny, but moist, and you bite into dark chocolate and dates! Yum! These muffins are very moist when just taken from the oven, but firm up on standing, and remain moist for several days.

Preheat the oven to 400°F. Oil 12 muffin cups.

Soak the bran and milk together in a medium bowl for 15 minutes. Meanwhile, mix the Dry Mixture ingredients together in a small bowl. Stir in the chopped dates and chocolate chips. Set aside.

Process the water and flaxseeds, then add the remaining Wet Mixture ingredients to the blender and process again for a minute.

Add the Wet Mix to the bowl of soaked bran, stirring briefly. Dump in the Dry Mix and stir briefly. Scoop evenly into the prepared muffin tin. Bake 20 minutes.

Loosen the muffins carefully with a table knife and set them on their sides in their muffin cups. Place the tin on a rack and

1½ cups wheat bran
1½ cups nondairy milk

DRY MIXTURE

1 cup whole wheat pastry flour
1 tablespoon baking powder
½ teaspoon salt

1 cup chopped pitted dates
½ cup semisweet chocolate chips

WET MIXTURE

¼ cup water and 1 tablespoon flaxseeds ground in blender (p. 183)
⅔ cup brown sugar or Sucanat
¼ cup unsweetened applesauce
2 tablespoons oil
½ tablespoon powdered egg replacer

let sit for at least 10 minutes before serving. Cool thoroughly and store in a closed plastic bag or container. They will keep moist for 2 or 3 days. These freeze well.

PER SERVING: each

Calories	217	FIBER	6.2g
Total Fat	6g	Carbohydrate	41g
Saturated Fat	2g	Protein	5g
Calories from fat	24%	Sodium	192mg

PEANUT BUTTER-BANANA BRAN MUFFINS

Makes 12 muffins

All you need is a little jam or jelly on these delicious muffins!

Preheat the oven to 375°F. Oil 12 muffin cups.

In a medium bowl, mix the Dry Mixture.

Process the water and flaxseeds, then add the remaining Wet Mixture ingredients to the blender and process again for a minute.

Pour the Wet Mix into the Dry Mix, and stir just until mixed. Spoon the batter into the prepared pan. Bake 20 minutes.

Loosen muffins carefully with a table knife, and set them on their sides in the muffins cups. Place the muffin pan on a rack, cover the muffins with a clean tea towel, and cool for a few minutes before serving. Cool thoroughly before storing in a plastic bag or container. These freeze well.

DRY MIXTURE
1½ cups whole wheat pastry flour

½ cup wheat bran

2 teaspoons baking powder

½ teaspoon salt

WET MIXTURE
½ cup water and 2 tablespoons flaxseeds ground in blender (p. 183)

1 cup mashed ripe banana (about 2 medium)

½ cup packed brown sugar or Sucanat

½ cup chunky natural peanut butter

½ cup nondairy milk

PEANUT BUTTER AND JELLY BRAN MUFFINS: Fill half of each muffin cup with batter. Spoon about 2 tablespoons of your favorite jam or jelly onto the batter. Top with the remaining batter and bake as above.

PER SERVING:			
Calories	192	FIBER	4.6g
Total Fat	6g	Carbohydrate	29g
Saturated Fat	1g	Protein	7g
Calories from fat	28%	Sodium	179mg

PEACH MELBA MUFFINS

Makes 12 muffins

Peach Melba is a popular dessert from the early 1900s. It was named after Nellie Melba, a famous opera singer of the day, and consisted of a raspberry sauce over peaches. This delicious muffin uses the same combination, and benefits from the high fiber content of the raspberries.

Preheat the oven to 400°F. Oil 12 muffin cups.

Mix the Dry Mix ingredients together in a medium bowl. Stir in the fruit; set aside.

Process the water and flaxseeds, then add the remaining Wet Mixture ingredients to the blender and process again for a minute.

Mix all of the Crumb Topping ingredients in a small bowl, rubbing the maple syrup in with your fingers, until crumbly.

Add the wet ingredients to dry ingredients, stirring briefly. Scoop evenly into the prepared muffin pan. Sprinkle the tops of the muffins generously and evenly with the Crumb Topping, patting it down gently into the batter. Bake 20 minutes. Loosen the muffins carefully with a table knife and set them on their sides in their muffin cups. Place the pan on a rack. Let sit 10 minutes before serving.

Cool completely and store in a plastic bag or container. These freeze well.

DRY MIXTURE
2 cups whole wheat pastry flour
2 teaspoons baking powder
½ teaspoon salt

FRUIT
¾ cup chopped ripe, peeled peaches
¾ cup fresh or frozen raspberries

WET MIXTURE
¼ cup water and 1 tablespoon flaxseeds ground in blender (p. 183)
¾ cup nondairy milk
⅓ cup sugar
¼ cup unsweetened applesauce
2 tablespoons oil or melted nondairy margarine
½ tablespoon powdered egg replacer
¼ teaspoon almond extract

CRUMB TOPPING
⅓ cup sugar
⅓ cup whole grain flour
1 tablespoon maple syrup
¼ cup chopped toasted almonds (optional)

PER SERVING:			
Calories	179	FIBER	4.3g
Total Fat	4g	Carbohydrate	32g
Saturated Fat	0g	Protein	5g
Calories from fat	20%	Sodium	155mg

CREAMY CORN MUFFINS

Makes 12 muffins

These are a favorite of mine, because I love anything corny, and these are double-corny! The stone-ground cornmeal contains more fiber than the ordinary refined type. The creamed corn (which actually contains no cream) adds more fiber, and makes the muffins moist and sweet.

Preheat the oven to 375°F. Oil 12 muffin cups.

Mix the Dry Mix ingredients together well in a medium bowl. Blend the Wet Mix ingredients in a blender. Pour the contents of the can of creamed corn into a smaller bowl. Pour the blended Wet Mix into the corn and stir well. Pour this mixture into the Dry Mix and mix briefly. Spoon evenly into the muffin tin. Bake 20 minutes.

Loosen the muffins carefully with a table knife and set them on their sides in their muffin cups. Place the pan on a rack, cover with a clean tea towel and cool for a few minutes before serving. Cool thoroughly before storing in a plastic bag container. These freeze well.

DRY MIXTURE

1 cup whole wheat pastry flour

1 cup stone-ground cornmeal

½ tablespoon baking powder

½ teaspoon salt

¼ teaspoon baking soda

WET MIXTURE

¾ cup nondairy milk

1 tablespoon oil or melted nondairy margarine

½ tablespoon powdered egg replacer

1 (14-ounce) can creamed corn

PER SERVING:			
Calories	115	FIBER	2.6g
Total Fat	2g	Carbohydrate	20g
Saturated Fat	0g	Protein	4g
Calories from fat	15%	Sodium	141mg

LEMON-WALNUT-BLUEBERRY MUFFINS

Makes 12 muffins

I like the addition of lemon zest in these delicate muffins. Blueberry muffins are usually a nutritional write-off, made from bleached white flour. These muffins are tender and light, and fiber-rich.

Preheat oven to 400°F. Oil 12 muffin cups.

Blend the wet ingredients in a blender. Mix the dry ingredients in a bowl. Add the fruit and nuts to the dry ingredients and toss. Add the wet ingredients and mix briefly. Spoon evenly into muffin cups. Sprinkle tops generously with brown sugar. Bake 20 minutes. Loosen muffins carefully with a knife and turn on their sides in cups. Place pan on a rack. Cool 10 minutes before serving.

WET MIXTURE

1¼ cups nondairy milk

¼ cup oil

2 tablespoons water

½ tablespoon powdered egg replacer

¾ cup sugar

Grated zest of 1 large lemon

DRY MIXTURE

2 cups whole wheat pastry flour

2 teaspoons baking powder

¾-1 teaspoon salt

¼ teaspoon freshly grated nutmeg

FRUIT AND NUTS

1 cup fresh or frozen blueberries

½ cup chopped walnuts

Brown sugar or Sucanat
to sprinkle on top

PER SERVING:			
Calories	217	FIBER	3.6g
Total Fat	9g	Carbohydrate	30g
Saturated Fat	1g	Protein	5g
Calories from fat	37%	Sodium	201mg

MOIST APPLE MUFFINS

Makes 12-14 large muffins

These are sure to become year-round favorites.

Preheat the oven to 350°F. Oil 12-14 muffin cups.

Blend the tofu in a blender or food processor with the juice concentrate (or sugar, water, and lemon mixture) until smooth.

In a medium bowl, whisk together the flours, baking powder, baking soda, salt, and cinnamon. Stir in the grated apples. Add the blended ingredients and stir briefly. Spoon the batter into prepared pan. Bake 25 minutes.

Loosen muffins carefully with a table knife and turn them on their sides in the muffin cups. Place the muffin pan on a rack, cover the muffins with a clean tea towel, and cool for a few minutes before serving. Cool thoroughly before storing in a plastic bag or container. These freeze well.

PER SERVING:			
Calories	148	FIBER	3.6g
Total Fat	2g	Carbohydrate	27g
Saturated Fat	0g	Protein	6g
Calories from fat	12%	Sodium	358mg

WET MIXTURE

12 ounces medium-firm tofu OR
1 (12.3-ounce) box firm
or extra-firm SILKEN tofu

9 ounces (¾ of a large can) frozen
apple juice concentrate, thawed OR
¾ cup sugar plus ½ cup water
and 1½ teaspoons lemon juice

DRY MIXTURE

1⅞ cups whole wheat flour

½ cup plus 1 tablespoon oat flour
(rolled oats
ground fine in a DRY blender)

1½ teaspoons baking powder

1½ teaspoons baking soda

1 teaspoon salt

1 teaspoon cinnamon

2 large apples, unpeeled, grated

Quick Tip

CAUTION: If you use paper muffin or cupcake liners, spray them first with nonstick spray or oil from a pump sprayer. The paper sticks to fat-free batters if you do not take this precautionary measure.

Ready-Bake Bran Muffins

Makes 36 muffins

If you're a bran muffin fan, take a few minutes to mix up this batter, which can be kept refrigerated in a tightly covered container for up to two weeks. Then you can have fresh muffins at a moment's notice. I've been making some version of this eggless muffin for many years.

Pour the bran into a large bowl; add the soymilk, raisins, molasses, salt, and Sucanat. Set aside. In a separate, large bowl, mix the dry ingredients. Pour in the bran mixture and mix briefly. Store in a large, tightly covered container in the refrigerator for up to 2 weeks.

To bake, preheat the oven to 350°F. Oil muffin cups. Spoon the batter into prepared pans, filling each cup about ¾ full. Bake 20 minutes.

Loosen muffins carefully with a knife and turn them on their sides in the muffins cups. Place the muffin pan on a rack, cover the muffins with a clean tea towel, and cool for a few minutes before serving. (These muffins firm up as they cool.) Cool thoroughly before storing in a plastic bag or container. These freeze well.

4½ cups wheat bran

6 cups soymilk or other nondairy milk or 4½ cups nondairy milk plus 1½ cups applesauce

1½ cups raisins or other chopped, dried fruit (optional)

1½ cups light or dark molasses

1½ teaspoons salt

¾ cup sugar

DRY MIXTURE

3 cups whole wheat pastry flour

3 cups whole wheat flour or unbleached white flour

1 tablespoon baking soda

1 tablespoon baking powder

2 tablespoons cinnamon (optional)

NOTE: These muffins contain no added fat, but if you prefer a richer muffin, use 4½ cups nondairy milk, 1 cup applesauce, and ½ cup oil.

PER SERVING:			
Calories	149	FIBER	6.1g
Total Fat	2g	Carbohydrate	32g
Saturated Fat	0g	Protein	5g
Calories from fat	12%	Sodium	147mg

High Fiber
PIZZA DOUGH

Makes 2 (12 to 14-inch) pizzas, 6-8 servings

I don't care for whole wheat pizza crust—I find it heavy. So, I use unbleached flour and add bran and ground flaxseeds to the dough. I like to make it in the morning, let it rise once, and then refrigerate it until dinner. This seems to improve it—it gets puffy around the edges like a brick oven pizza.

1¼ cups lukewarm water

½ tablespoon regular baking yeast

½ teaspoon sugar

3¼ cups unbleached white flour

¼ cup wheat bran

3 tablespoons ground flaxseeds

1 tablespoon extra-virgin olive oil

½ tablespoon salt

In a medium bowl or bowl of a heavy-duty mixer, mix the water, yeast, and sugar. Let it stand until it gets frothy. Add 2 cups of the flour, the wheat bran, flaxseeds, oil, and salt and stir well. Add the remaining flour and knead for 5-8 minutes. Place the dough in an oiled bowl, cover, and let rise in a warm spot for an hour.

Punch the dough down and either use it right away, or cover it well with plastic wrap and place it in the refrigerator until you are ready to bake.

When you are ready to bake, preheat the oven (see oven temperature* at right) and punch down the dough. Divide the dough into 2 balls for a 12-inch pizza, or 5 balls for small pizzas. On a well-floured board, roll the dough out to fit your pans, or into five 4 to 6-inch pizzas, leaving a bit of a rim around the edge. Top your pizza as desired. See baking times at right.

*OVEN TEMPERATURE AND BAKING TIMES

You want the dough to cook fast, but not dry out, and you want the toppings to be juicy. I bake pizza very quickly in my electric stove's convection oven at 500°F, but experiment with your oven starting at 425°F.

At 500°F in a convection oven, pizza will cook in about 8 minutes. At a lower temperature with no convection, it may take 15 minutes. The bottom of the crust should be crispy and golden, with perhaps a few scorched spots, and the top should be bubbly and slightly browned, with a nice puffy edge. The crust should be chewy. Serve immediately, cutting into wedges with a sharp knife, a pizza cutter, or a pair of kitchen shears (my favorite).

PER SERVING:			
Calories	231	FIBER	3.3g
Total Fat	3g	Carbohydrate	42g
Saturated Fat	0g	Protein	7g
Calories from fat	11%	Sodium	457mg

Basic Tender 100%
WHOLE WHEAT BREAD

Makes 2 large loaves, 32 servings

In a small bowl, dissolve the yeast in ¾ cup warm water with sweetener. When frothy, add it to a large bowl, or the bowl of a heavy-duty mixer with a dough hook, along with the 2 cups of warm water, salt, oil, and 4 cups of the whole wheat flour (and the optional potato flour and/or soy flour, if using). Mix in the remaining 3 cups of flour, kneading by hand or in the heavy-duty mixer with dough hook 8-10 minutes. (If kneading by hand, use as little flour as possible, to ensure a moist bread. Use a little oil on your hands and the kneading surface, if necessary.) Transfer the dough to a large oiled bowl. Oil the top of the dough and cover with plastic wrap. Let rise in a warm place for 1½-2 hours. Punch down and let rise about 1½ hours more.

Oil two 9 x 5-inch loaf pans. Shape dough into 2 even loaves and place in loaf pans. Cover and let rise about 30-45 minutes, or until well-rounded over the tops of the pans. Meanwhile, preheat the oven to 350°F.

Just before baking, slash the tops of the loaves with a razor blade, if you like. Mist the loaves with water. Place in the middle of the oven. Bake 30 minutes. Remove from pans and cool on racks.

I teaspoon yeast
(not instant quick-rising)

¾ cup very warm water
or potato cooking water

I tablespoon sweetener of choice

2 cups warm water, potato
cooking water, or soymilk

I tablespoon salt

2 tablespoons oil

7 cups whole wheat flour

⅓ cup potato flour or potato starch
(not needed if using potato cooking
water) (optional)

⅓ cup soy flour (optional)

MULTI-GRAIN BREAD: Substitute any whole grain flour for up to 2½ cups of the flour.

PER SERVING:			
Calories	133	FIBER	4.4g
Total Fat	2g	Carbohydrate	26g
Saturated Fat	0g	Protein	5g
Calories from fat	13%	Sodium	268mg

No-Knead
BURGER BUNS

Makes 9-12 buns

This dough also can be used for dinner rolls, and other varieties of breads, too—see the variations.

Dissolve the yeast in the water. In a medium bowl, combine soymilk, potato flakes, oil, syrup, salt, and yeast flakes if using. Add yeast mixture, ground flaxseeds, and flour and stir 2 minutes; cover and let rise in a warm place for 30 minutes.

Oil 1-2 baking sheets and sprinkle with flour or cornmeal. Turn the dough out on a well-floured countertop and sprinkle with flour. With floured hands, form the dough into 9-12 equal-sized balls. Place on oiled baking sheets sprinkled with flour or cornmeal and pat the balls down to form 3 to 4-inch rounds. Press down in centers so balls don't form "humps" when they rise. Cover and let rise 30 minutes. Preheat the oven to 350°F.

Brush the buns with soymilk and sprinkle with sesame seeds or other topping. Bake 15 minutes. Cool on racks.

1 tablespoon yeast
(not instant quick-rising)

1 cup warm water

2 cups warm soymilk

¼ cup instant mashed potato flakes

2 tablespoons oil

2 tablespoons maple syrup or sugar

2 teaspoons salt

1 tablespoon nutritional yeast flakes
(optional)

¼ cup ground flaxseeds

4 cups whole wheat flour

Soymilk for glazing

Sesame seeds or other desired topping
(optional)

DINNER ROLLS: After the first rising, pat the dough out on a floured surface and cut rounds with a biscuit cutter. Place close together on an oiled baking pan, rise until doubled, and then bake 15 minutes. For shiny tops, brush the rolls with soymilk before baking.

You can also simply spoon the risen dough out into oiled muffin cups, rather than patting and cutting.

"HOT DOG" BUNS: Shape the dough into oblongs the length of the "weiners" you prefer.

PER SERVING:

Calories	245	FIBER	7.5g
Total Fat	6g	Carbohydrate	38g
Saturated Fat	1g	Protein	10g
Calories from fat	22%	Sodium	395mg

APPETIZERS AND SNACKS

Whole grain breads and crackers, fresh and dried fruits, nuts and seeds, and raw veggies make perfect high-fiber snacks and appetizers. But if you're looking for some more innovative ways to add fiber to your daily menus without adding lots of fat and sugar, read on. These are some of our favorite recipes, and ones that I often take to parties and potlucks.

CLASSIC ALMOND MUSHROOM PÂTÉ

Makes about 1½ cups

This type of vegetarian pâté appeared in mainstream magazines in the early 1980s and became deservedly popular party fare. I've modernized it by omitting the butter, using fewer almonds (still in their fiber-rich skins), and more mushrooms, and by using slightly more authoritative seasoning. It's delicious and easy to make.

½ medium onion, cut into chunks

1 large clove garlic, peeled

¾ pound fresh white or cremini (brown) mushrooms, cleaned and halved

¾ teaspoon salt

¼ teaspoon dried thyme or tarragon

⅛ teaspoon white pepper

1 cup almonds (shelled but still in skins), toasted*

1 tablespoon dry sherry, marsala, or madeira

Chopped fresh parsley and/or chopped toasted almonds (optional)

Process the onion and garlic in a food processor until finely chopped. Add the mushrooms through the top with the motor running and chop. Lightly oil a large nonstick frying pan and heat it over medium-high heat. Add the chopped vegetables, salt, thyme or tarragon, and pepper; cook, stirring frequently, until most of the liquid has evaporated. Remove from heat.

Place the toasted almonds in the food processor and process until they almost become a paste; scrape them from the sides of the bowl. Add the cooked mushroom mixture and the wine. Process until quite smooth. Pack into an oiled bowl, cover, and chill. When cool, invert on a plate. The pâté can be decorated with chopped fresh parsley or chopped toasted almonds.

Quick Tip

Toasting Almonds

*To toast the almonds, either place them in a heavy frying pan over medium-low heat and stir them frequently for about 5 to 7 minutes, or spread them on a microwave-safe plate, leaving a space in the center of the plate, and microwave on HIGH for 3 minutes. Stir them a bit, again leaving a space in the center, and microwave 2 more minutes.

PER SERVING: 2 tablespoons			
Calories	86	FIBER	1.8g
Total Fat	7g	Carbohydrate	5g
Saturated Fat	1g	Protein	3g
Calories from fat	73%	Sodium	136mg

HERBED VEGGIE PÂTÉ

Makes two 3 x 6 x 2-inch loaves (16 servings)

This delicious pâté (high-fat versions of which are for sale in most health food stores) is versatile and very easy to make. It makes an excellent spread on celery sticks, crackers, rye crisp, melba toast, or regular toast; an elegant starter when served with crusty French bread on a bed of lettuce; or scrumptious sandwich material.

Preheat the oven to 350° F. Combine all of the ingredients in a blender or food processor and blend until very smooth. Divide the mixture between 2 lightly oiled nonstick 3 x 6 x 2-inch loaf pans. Cover each pan with foil. Place the pans inside a 9 x 13-inch shallow baking pan with about 1 inch of hot water in the bottom. Bake for 1 hour, removing the foil during the last 20 minutes of baking. Cool on a wire rack. Carefully loosen the edges with a knife and invert loaves onto plates. Serve immediately or wrap and refrigerate up to 1 week. To freeze, cut loaves into whatever sizes are useful for you, and wrap well with foil, then plastic. Can be frozen up to 3 months.

½ cup warm water

1 medium onion (about 5 ounces), peeled and cut into chunks

1 large russet potato (about 8 ounces), scrubbed and cut into chunks*

1 cup raw shelled walnuts, hazelnuts, almonds, cashews, pecans, sunflower seeds, or a mixture

½ cup whole wheat flour, stone-ground cornmeal, soy flour, or chickpea flour (besan)

½ cup nutritional yeast flakes

½ cup soy sauce

2-4 cloves garlic, peeled

½-1 teaspoon each dried thyme, dried rosemary, and dried marjoram

¼ teaspoon ground allspice (optional)

A few gratings fresh nutmeg

Freshly ground black pepper to taste

POSSIBLE SUBSTITUTIONS

1 small potato (4 ounces) AND 1 medium-large carrot, both scrubbed and cut into chunks

1 tablespoon each fresh herbs, chopped fine

PER SERVING:			
Calories	95	FIBER	1.3g
Total Fat	5g	Carbohydrate	10g
Saturated Fat	0g	Protein	5g
Calories from fat	47%	Sodium	50mg

Miso Pâté

Makes about 2 cups

I've been making this spread, adapted from The Book of Miso, *for many years. It is much more delicious than its ingredients suggest, and tastes a bit like liverwurst, so it's great on crackers or rye or French bread. For the breadcrumbs, use a light whole wheat bread.*

2 cups fresh soft whole wheat breadcrumbs* (See ingredient note)

½ cup water

4 green onions, chopped

1 clove garlic, crushed or minced

¼ cup tahini

2½ tablespoons light miso

Pinch each dried thyme, rosemary, and sage

Roasted (Asian) sesame oil or extra-virgin olive oil (optional)

In a small bowl, mash the breadcrumbs and water together with a fork until the crumbs absorb all the water. Mince the onions and garlic in a food processor. Add the remaining ingredients except the oil and process just until everything is mixed. (Don't process too long or the mixture will become gummy.) Pack into a small serving bowl and cover. Refrigerate for at least 1 hour and preferably overnight before serving. If you like, drizzle with a little roasted (Asian) sesame oil or extra-virgin olive oil before serving.

*INGREDIENT NOTE: Use a light-textured whole wheat bread for the crumbs, not a really heavy one.

PER SERVING: 2 tablespoons			
Calories	95	FIBER	1.3g
Total Fat	5g	Carbohydrate	10g
Saturated Fat	0g	Protein	5g
Calories from fat	47%	Sodium	50mg

— Quick Snack —

Roasted Soybeans/Chickpeas

Keep a supply of these on hand to make a lower-fat, high-fiber alternative to roasted nuts for munching. Soak dry soybeans or chickpeas overnight in enough water to cover generously. Drain, rinse, and place in a pot with fresh water to cover. Bring to a boil, reduce heat, and simmer, covered, 10 minutes. Drain.

Preheat the oven to 350°F. Spread the beans in a single layer on lightly oiled cookie sheets. Spray with oil. Sprinkle with salt or a seasoned or herbal salt mixture. Roast the beans for about 45 minutes, stirring often, until golden and crispy all over. Cool completely, and store in plastic bags, plastic containers, or glass jars. Freeze for long-term storage.

MUHAMMARA
(Turkish Red Pepper Walnut and Garlic Spread with Pomegranate Molasses)

Makes about 2 cups

This exquisite spread uses a small amount of pomegranate molasses, a common ingredient in Middle Eastern and Eastern Mediterranean cooking. It is essentially reduced pomegranate juice and has a very tart yet sweet flavor. Buy it in Middle Eastern groceries (it's inexpensive). It's called "Dibs Roumman"; Cedar is a common brand. Once you taste it, you'll find all sorts of uses for it—in marinades and glazes, salad dressings, etc. Another plus: It keeps a long time in the refrigerator.

2 large sweet red bell peppers or good-quality jarred roasted red peppers, rinsed

1 tablespoon water

⅔ cup walnuts (preferably lightly toasted)

1 tablespoon crushed garlic

⅔ cup toasted or semi-dried whole wheat breadcrumbs*

¼ cup extra-virgin olive oil

1½ teaspoons ground cumin

½ teaspoon red pepper flakes

2 teaspoons pomegranate molasses

2 tablespoons fresh lemon juice

½ teaspoon salt

Roast the peppers under the broiler or on a grill until charred all over. Place them in a paper bag; seal and set aside for 10 minutes. Peel, stem, and seed the peppers, then chop coarsely.

Place all of the ingredients in the food processor and process until quite smooth. Taste for salt. Let stand several hours before serving. If chilled, bring to room temperature before serving.

*NOTE: Use a light-textured whole wheat bread for the crumbs, not a really heavy bread.

SERVING TIP: Serve this spread with sesame crackers or any Arabic flatbread, such as pita and pita crisps, or raw vegetables.

PER SERVING: 2 tablespoons			
Calories	67	FIBER	0.5g
Total Fat	6g	Carbohydrate	2g
Saturated Fat	1g	Protein	1g
Calories from fat	80%	Sodium	72mg

PERSIAN-STYLE HUMMUS WITH GREENS

Makes about 3½ cups

Most versions of this popular Middle Eastern chickpea dip are chock-full of olive oil and tahini. This one has just a little tahini; you can drizzle a little extra-virgin olive oil over the top, if you like. But it has lots of spinach, which adds even more fiber and nutrition, and lots of color. If you like, you can substitute other greens, such as kale or chard, for the spinach. Serve with wedges of whole wheat pita bread.

2 cups well-cooked or canned chickpeas, drained

⅓ cup lemon juice

2 tablespoons tahini

6 cloves garlic, peeled

1½ tsp. salt

1 teaspoon ground cumin

¼ teaspoon cayenne pepper

1 (10-ounce) package frozen chopped spinach, thawed; or 1 pound fresh spinach, steamed until tender

Place all of the ingredients except the spinach in a food processor. Process until smooth, adding a bit of water or chickpea liquid if necessary. Squeeze the spinach to remove as much liquid as possible. Add the spinach to the chickpea mixture and process briefly. Place in a serving bowl, cover with plastic wrap and refrigerate until serving time.

NOTE: Hummus will thicken in the refrigerator. It can be thinned with a little water or chickpea liquid.

PER SERVING: ¼ cup			
Calories	60	FIBER	2.2g
Total Fat	2g	Carbohydrate	9g
Saturated Fat	0g	Protein	3g
Calories from fat	30%	Sodium	249mg

VARIATION

For traditional hummus, omit the spinach and decrease the salt to 1 teaspoon, the cumin to ½ teaspoon, and the cayenne to a pinch.

CYPRIOT DILL AND "FAVA" SPREAD

Makes about 2½ cups

The quotation marks are for the simple reason that this spread isn't really made with fava beans, but it tastes like it is! Dried fava beans can be hard to find in some areas and are difficult to peel and sometimes expensive. Fortunately, dried split yellow peas taste very similar and are cheap and readily available. Oddly enough, in Cyprus and in Greece, split yellow peas are called "fava"!

3 cups water

1 cup dried split yellow peas

½ medium onion, peeled and cut into chunks

6 cloves garlic, peeled

1 teaspoon salt

2 tablespoons fresh lemon juice

1 tablespoon extra-virgin olive oil

2 teaspoons dried dillweed or 2 tablespoons fresh dillweed

Freshly ground black pepper to taste

Olive oil, sprig fresh dillweed or paprika for garnish (optional)

Combine the water, peas, onion, garlic, and salt in a medium saucepan. Bring to a boil, skimming off any foam. Reduce heat to a simmer, cover, and cook 30 minutes. Pour into a food processor and process with the remaining ingredients, except garnishes, until smooth, leaving the "pusher" out of the top of the food processor so that hot air can escape from the bowl while you work. Pour into a decorative serving bowl, cover, and refrigerate. Can be served cool or at room temperature. Before serving, you may like to drizzle a little olive oil on top and decorate with a sprig of fresh dill or some paprika.

SERVING TIP: This spread is delicious with whole wheat pita crisps or sesame crackers.

PER SERVING: 2 tablespoons			
Calories	37	FIBER	2g
Total Fat	1g	Carbohydrate	5g
Saturated Fat	0g	Protein	2g
Calories from fat	24%	Sodium	107mg

CANNELLINI SPREAD
with Sun-Dried Tomatoes or Roasted Red Peppers

Makes about 2 cups

This spread is a wonderful party food and makes an elegant change from hummus. Serve warm or at room temperature with rye or other crackers, pita or bagel crisps, slices of fresh crusty French bread or crostini, breadsticks, or raw vegetables.

Heat a heavy, preferably nonstick, skillet over high heat. Add the onion and garlic and stir-fry, adding just enough broth from time to time to keep the onions from sticking. When the onions are soft and as brown as you like them, place them in a food processor with all of the remaining ingredients except optional garnishes and process until almost smooth. If using jarred roasted red peppers, be sure to rinse them well before adding to the other ingredients. Pack into a serving bowl, cover and refrigerate until serving time.

To serve the dip hot, place it in a heat-proof bowl, cover, and microwave for a couple of minutes, or heat in a 250-300°F oven until heated through. Before serving, you may wish to drizzle a little extra-virgin olive oil over the top and sprinkle with chopped fresh parsley or other fresh herbs.

1 large onion, minced

2 large cloves garlic, minced

½ cup vegetable broth

1 (15-oz.) can or 1½ cups cooked cannellini (white kidney) beans

½ cup sun-dried tomatoes in oil, rinsed in hot water, well-drained, and patted dry with paper towels OR ½ cup roasted red peppers

1½ tablespoons fresh lemon juice or white wine vinegar

2 tablespoons minced fresh parsley (preferably Italian parsley)

½ to ¾ teaspoon salt

½ teaspoon each dried thyme and basil or ½ to ¾ teaspoon each fresh, chopped thyme and basil or other favorite herbs

White pepper to taste

OPTIONAL
Extra-virgin olive oil and/or chopped fresh parsley or other herbs for garnish

PER SERVING: ¼ cup			
Calories	66	FIBER	2.6g
Total Fat	0g	Carbohydrate	13g
Saturated Fat	0g	Protein	4g
Calories from fat	0%	Sodium	248mg

SPICY MEXICAN BEAN DIP
(or "Refried Beans")

Makes 3½-4 cups

This fat-free dip gets its light texture from being whirled for several minutes in the food processor. It can be made with black, red, or pinto beans, and it's good hot or cold. It also makes a great low-fat stand-in for "refried" beans in any Mexican or Southwestern dish.

3 (15-ounce) cans (4½ cups cooked) black, small red, or pinto beans, drained

1 small onion, minced

2 tablespoons cider or red wine vinegar

1 teaspoon salt

1 teaspoon ground cumin

1 teaspoon dried oregano

3 cloves garlic, crushed OR 1 teaspoon garlic granules or powder

1 teaspoon chile powder

Red pepper sauce to taste, plus a dash of liquid smoke OR 2 teaspoons pureed canned chile chipotle in adobado sauce

Place all of the ingredients in a food processor and blend until very smooth. (This will take several minutes.) Place in a serving bowl, cover, and refrigerate.

TO SERVE THE DIP HOT, heat the dip in the microwave on HIGH for about 3 minutes, or in a skillet, stirring constantly, until heated through.

TIP: You may use any kind of chile powder in this recipe, but try some of the more exotic, dark varieties for a richer flavor.

PER SERVING: ¼ cup			
Calories	72	FIBER	4.7g
Total Fat	0g	Carbohydrate	13g
Saturated Fat	0g	Protein	5g
Calories from fat	0%	Sodium	143mg

Quick Snack

Green Soybeans in the pod (Edamamé)

This is a favorite snack in Japan and China, and it is addictive! Green soybeans are delicious and nutty-tasting. Look for green soybeans frozen in the pod in Asian or Japanese markets and in many natural food stores and supermarkets.

Boil or steam the fresh or frozen pods of green soybeans for about 20 minutes. Drain and serve warm. Everyone salts his own portion. Place a pod in your mouth and close your teeth over the end, holding on to the tip of the pod with your fingers. Keeping your teeth closed, pull the pod out of your mouth. The beans will pop out into your mouth. Discard the pods. Repeat.

Salsa Cruda con Olive
(Italian Raw Tomato Sauce with Black Olives)

Makes about 2 cups

This is a delicious topping for bruschetta, but it can also be served with crackers or even over pasta.

IF YOU HAVE NO FOOD PROCESSOR, chop the tomatoes quite small, and mince the onions and olives. Mix tomatoes, onions, and olives in a small bowl with the basil and salt and pepper to taste (and any optional additions desired). Cover and chill until serving time.

IF YOU HAVE A FOOD PROCESSOR, pulse the onion and olives a few times to mince them, then add the chunked tomato and pulse until coarsely chopped. Pour into the bowl and toss with the basil, salt and pepper to taste, and any optionals you are using.

PER SERVING: ¼ cup

Calories	46	FIBER	1.8g
Total Fat	2g	Carbohydrate	7g
Saturated Fat	0g	Protein	1g
Calories from fat	39%	Sodium	283mg

---

2 pounds firm ripe Roma (plum) tomatoes, cut into chunks

40 black kalamata olives, pitted*

6 cloves garlic, crushed

6 tablespoons chopped fresh basil

½ teaspoon salt

Freshly ground black pepper to taste

OPTIONAL ADDITIONS

2-4 tablespoons extra-virgin olive oil

1 red or sweet onion, chopped fine

½ cup minced fresh Italian parsley

½-1 cup chopped marinated artichoke hearts

---

*It's the Pits!

There is nothing difficult about pitting olives—you use the same procedure as peeling a clove of garlic: Simply place the olive on a cutting board. Place the wide part of a chef's knife horizontally on the olive. Strike the flat of the knife with your fist, and the pit practically pops out.

Poor Man's Caviar

Makes about 2 cups

Try serving this spread in small crêpes, or on whole grain crackers.

Process the garlic in the food processor until finely minced before adding anything else. Add the olives, miso, water, oil, and salt, and process until a rough paste forms. Add the quinoa and pulse until the mixture is chopped up a bit, but you don't want a paste—it should have some texture. Spoon into a serving bowl, stir in the white part of the onions, then sprinkle the green part on top. Serve immediately, or cover and chill.

I clove garlic

I cup pitted, sliced California ripe olives

I tablespoon miso

I tablespoon water

I tablespoon extra-virgin olive oil

White part of 2 green onions, minced

¼ teaspoon salt

1½ cups cooked, chilled quinoa

Green part of 2 green onions,
finely sliced, for garnish

COOKING QUINOA

Most quinoa that you buy now has been rinsed to rid it of the natural saponins that coat it, but you should put it into a sieve and rinse it under cold running water just to be sure. Drain well. Quinoa is better if you toast it a bit in a dry heavy skillet over medium heat for a few minutes, but you can skip that step.

For this recipe, add ½ cup quinoa (prepared as above) to 1 cup boiling water in a small saucepan with a pinch or two of salt. Bring to a boil, then turn down, cover, and cook for 15-20 minutes, or until the water is absorbed. Let stand off the heat for 10 minutes. For this recipe, it should be refrigerated first.

PER SERVING: ¼ cup

Calories	89	FIBER	1.7g
Total Fat	5g	Carbohydrate	8g
Saturated Fat	1g	Protein	2g
Calories from fat	50%	Sodium	273mg

SALADS, DRESSINGS AND SAUCES

Salads can give you scope for some of the greatest quick, high-fiber meals. You can use whatever you have around, whaever's in season, whatever sounds good to you. You can use the dressing recipes and ideas here for your own full-meal or side salads, or check out some of my favorite recipes. Cooks are getting more and more experimental with salads, using whole grains, pastas, breads, legumes, and exotic fruits and vegetables—all possibilities for delicious, high-fiber eating!

There are no ironclad rules for salads, except that the greens be very fresh—the best you can pick or buy.

The dressings in this section are not limited to salad toppings. They're great on beans and whole grains as well. The Bechamel sauce at the end of the chapter is excellent on cooked vegetables.

Italian Wine Vinegar Dressing

(Basic Vinaigrette)

Makes a generous ⅓ cup (4 servings)

This is a basic formula for an Italian-style salad dressing. Forget those gloppy store-bought messes made with stale herbs! Remember that you can leave out the garlic if you don't like it, and that freshly ground pepper and chopped fresh herbs are optionals that you can sprinkle over the salad while dressing it. This method of mixing is easy and convenient for small amounts made just before dressing the salad.

With the back of a teaspoon in a small round-bottomed bowl, or with a mortar and pestle, mash together the salt and garlic to make a paste. (The salt grains will help mash the garlic to a paste and the garlic juice will dissolve the salt.) Whisk in the oil, any broth you are using, and vinegar with a fork or small whisk.

¼ teaspoon salt

I small clove garlic, crushed or minced

5 tablespoons extra-virgin olive oil*

I tablespoon good-quality red wine vinegar or white balsamic vinegar

I teaspoon balsamic vinegar (red or white)

*TO REDUCE FAT AND CALORIES, use one of the oil substitutes on page 67 for up to ¼ cup of the olive oil—I usually use chickpea cooking broth—but use at least 1 tablespoon of olive oil.

PER SERVING:			
Calories	149	FIBER	0g
Total Fat	17g	Carbohydrate	0g
Saturated Fat	2g	Protein	0g
Calories from fat	45%	Sodium	133mg

Quick Tip

Mixing Dressings

If you want to multiply this or another dressing recipe, a good method of mixing larger amounts of dressing is to place all of the ingredients (using crushed garlic) in a Tupperware Quick-Shake® container, or a jar with a tight cover, and shake until well mixed.

No-Fat Oil Substitutes
for Salad Dressings

Makes I cup

Use this simple mixture in place of all or some of the oil in salad dressing.

Mix together in a small saucepan. Cook, stirring constantly, until thickened and clear. If using cornstarch, the mixture must be brought to a boil; a potato starch mixture does not need to be.

I cup cold water
or light vegetable broth

2 teaspoon cornstarch
or potato starch

OTHER OIL SUBSTITUTES

If you prefer, you can use cold potato cooking water, or broth from cooking chickpeas (which jells when cool), or white kidney (cannellini) beans instead of the starch mixture. Other options might be tomato juice or vegetable juice cocktail, or other freshly extracted vegetable and fruit juices. If the dressing needs some thickening, use puréed fruit, puréed cooked beans or vegetables, roasted garlic, a bit of blended silken or soft tofu, blended raw cashews, or commercial low-fat mayonnaise.

Homemade Dressings

I use a variety of homemade low-oil and sometimes oil-free dressings, but there are some acceptable commercial ones on the market now. If you prefer homemade dressings but want to make them lower in fat, you can use my Substitute Salad Dressings or the broth from cooking potatoes, chickpeas, or white kidney (cannellini) beans in your recipes. Feel free to change the proportions and seasonings in my recipes to suit your taste. Use some of those delicious gourmet herbal and fruit vinegars you might have received as gifts to give winter salads a lift.

Cold cooked vegetables dressed with vinegar or lemon juice and olive oil qualify as salads, and make beautiful additions to a buffet table when arranged artistically on platters. Almost any fresh, seasonal vegetable can be treated this way: Simply cook, steam, roast, or grill until just tender and drizzle with a little extra-virgin olive oil and lemon juice or one of the many vinegar varieties, such as red wine vinegar or white or red balsamic vinegar. Sprinkle with salt and freshly ground pepper. Herbs can be used to garnish the dish. You can treat artichokes, asparagus, green beans, carrots, fennel, mushrooms, fresh fava or broad beans, cooked chard or other greens (such as beet tops), cauliflower, broccoli, roasted peppers, and onions this way.

BALSAMIC VINAIGRETTE

Makes 1½ cups

This is one of my favorite dressings. It keeps for several weeks in the refrigerator—just shake it a little before serving.

1 cup water or light broth

2 teaspoons cornstarch or potato starch

¼ cup extra-virgin olive oil

½ cup plus 2 tablespoons balsamic vinegar (⅔ cup total)

1 to 3 cloves garlic, crushed

1⅝ teaspoons salt or 2⅛ teaspoons herbal salt

2½ tablespoons brown sugar or Sucanat (optional)

Place the water or broth and starch in a small saucepan and stir over high heat until it thickens and turns clear (cornstarch has to boil; potato starch does not). Whisk or blend in the remaining ingredients, bottle and store in the refrigerator.

DIJON-BALSAMIC VINAIGRETTE: Reduce the salt by half and add 1½ tablespoons Dijon mustard and 1 green onion, chopped (optional).

CREAMY BALSAMIC VINAIGRETTE: Add ⅓ cup of your favorite low-fat mayonnaise.

PER SERVING: 1 tablespoon

Calories	22	FIBER	0g
Total Fat	2g	Carbohydrate	0g
Saturated Fat	0g	Protein	0g
Calories from fat	81%	Sodium	144mg

Quick Tip

Cole Slaw & Carrot Salads

The Easy Coleslaw or Carrot Salad Dressing (page 69) is the one I use most often on this type of salad, but try any favorite creamy or vinaigrette dressing. Asian seasonings and vinegars also suit these vegetables (see Thai Cabbage Salad on page 75).

For a presentation that lifts these salads from the ordinary to the sublime, place each serving of salad on a red cabbage leaf, and garnish with parsley or cilantro and citrus wedges.

My Mother's Lemon and Olive Oil Salad Dressing

Makes a scant ½ cup (4 servings)

My mother never buys prepared salad dressing. This is my version of the one we had on our big daily bowl of salad greens when I was growing up. She also never measures ingredients, but I have figured out a formula for those who like to use exact amounts. This method of mixing is easy and convenient for small amounts made just before dressing the salad.

With the back of a teaspoon in a small round-bottomed bowl, or with a mortar and pestle, mash together the salt and garlic to make a paste. (The salt grains will help mash the garlic to a paste and the garlic juice will dissolve the salt.) Whisk in the oil, any broth you are using, and vinegar with a fork or small whisk. (See mixing dressings tip, page 66.)

¼ teaspoon salt
1 small clove garlic, minced or crushed
5 tablespoons extra-virgin olive oil*
2 tablespoons fresh lemon juice

*TO REDUCE FAT AND CALORIES, use one of the oil substitutes on page 67 for up to ¼ cup of the olive oil—I usually use chickpea cooking broth—but use at least 1 tablespoon of olive oil.

PER SERVING:			
Calories	151	FIBER	0g
Total Fat	17g	Carbohydrate	1g
Saturated Fat	2g	Protein	0g
Calories from fat	45%	Sodium	133mg

Quick Tip

Easy Coleslaw or Carrot Salad Dressing

Mix your favorite low-fat mayonnaise with any kind of fruit juice (try some of the more exotic combinations) until it is thin enough and sweet enough to suit your taste. Flavor with herbs and/or spices, if you wish.

Not-So-Sweet Four Bean Salad

Makes 6 servings

You can make this delicious salad quickly and keep it for up to a week in the refrigerator for quick lunches or as a hearty addition to a green salad. It's oil-free and contains much less sugar than the traditional bean salad. It's always a hit at potlucks. If you'd like to use some oil in this salad, use only ¾ cup of the cornstarch mixture or chickpea broth, and ¼ cup extra-virgin olive oil.

Mix the salad ingredients in a serving bowl.

Place the water or broth and starch in a small saucepan and stir over high heat until it thickens and turns clear. (Cornstarch has to boil; potato starch does not.) Whisk or blend in the remaining ingredients. Pour hot dressing over the salad ingredients. Cover and refrigerate until serving time, shaking or stirring daily.

PASTA-BEAN SALAD: Reduce beans by half and substitute 3 cups cooked whole grain spiral or tube pasta. Use chopped bell pepper instead of celery, if you like.

SALAD

1 (15-ounce) can or 1½ cups cooked chickpeas, drained

1 (15-ounce) can or 1½ cups cooked small red beans or kidney beans, drained

1 (15-ounce) can or 1½ cups cooked black-eyed peas, drained

1½ cups cooked fresh or frozen small, whole green beans, drained

1 cup diced celery

3 green onions, chopped

⅓ cup minced fresh parsley

SWEET AND SOUR DRESSING

1 cup cold water or vegetable broth

2 teaspoons cornstarch or potato starch

⅔ cup red wine vinegar

3 tablespoons maple syrup

3 cloves garlic, crushed

2 teaspoons salt

1 teaspoon pepper

1 teaspoon dry mustard

1 teaspoon vegetarian Worcestershire sauce (optional)

PER SERVING:			
Calories	221	FIBER	9.5g
Total Fat	2g	Carbohydrate	42g
Saturated Fat	0g	Protein	12g
Calories from fat	8%	Sodium	739mg

ITALIAN-STYLE BEAN SALAD

Makes 6 servings

If you refrigerate this salad, bring it to room temperature before serving.

Warm the beans slightly in their liquid, then drain well. Place beans in a serving bowl. Blend the oil, broth, vinegar, miso, green onion, and sage or basil until creamy; pour over the beans. Add the parsley and salt and pepper to taste and mix well.

NOTE: Don't use the liquid from canned beans in this recipe.

3 cups cooked or 2 (15-ounce) cans cannellini (white kidney beans) or Great Northern beans

3 tablespoons extra-virgin olive oil

3 tablespoons vegetable broth or chickpea or cannellini cooking broth

1 tablespoon red wine vinegar

2 teaspoons light miso

1 green onion, chopped

1 tablespoon chopped fresh sage or basil

¼ cup chopped Italian parsley

Salt and freshly ground black pepper to taste

Other Italian-Style Bean Salads

1.) Dress cooked or canned romano, borlotti, cranberry, or pinto beans with Italian Wine Vinegar Dressing (page 66), and serve with strips of radicchio or curly endive.

2.) Dress cooked or canned chickpeas or brown lentils with My Mother's Lemon Dressing (page 69) or Italian Wine Vinegar Dressing (page 66). Mix with chopped green or red onions and chopped fresh Italian parsley.

PER SERVING:			
Calories	169	FIBER	6.4g
Total Fat	7g	Carbohydrate	20g
Saturated Fat	1g	Protein	8g
Calories from fat	37%	Sodium	73mg

Pasta Primavera Salad

Makes 6-8 servings

Here's a hearty full-meal salad that's good enough to serve to company.

Cook the pasta according to package directions. Meanwhile, prepare the vegetables. If using fresh carrots, add them to the pot with the pasta when the pasta is about half cooked. If using frozen carrots, add them with the green beans to the pot when the pasta is almost tender. When the pasta is just tender but still chewy, drain in a colander with the carrots and green beans.

Place the drained pasta and vegetables in a large serving bowl with the onion, beans, peppers, and celery. Add 2 tablespoons vinegar, 1 teaspoon salt, and pepper to taste; toss well.

Blend all of the dressing ingredients in a blender or food processor until very smooth. Pour it over the warm pasta and combine well. Cover and refrigerate. Serve cold or at room temperature.

SALAD

¾ pound uncooked whole grain rotelle or fusilli (corkscrew) pasta

2 medium carrots, scrubbed and cut into thin oval slices or 3 cups frozen sliced carrots

½ pound frozen whole small green beans

1 large onion, chopped

1 (15-ounce) can or 1½ cups cooked white kidney (cannellini) beans OR chickpeas, drained

1 green bell pepper, seeded and diced

1 red bell pepper, seeded and diced

1 cup thinly sliced celery

2 tablespoons white wine vinegar

1 teaspoon salt

Freshly ground black pepper to taste

CREAMY BASIL DRESSING

1⅓ cups firm or extra-firm SILKEN tofu

¼ cup lemon juice

¼ cup chopped fresh basil or 1½ tablespoons dried basil

1 tablespoon white wine vinegar

1 teaspoon salt

½ teaspoon dry mustard powder

PER SERVING:			
Calories	357	FIBER	9.8g
Total Fat	3g	Carbohydrate	66g
Saturated Fat	0g	Protein	19g
Calories from fat	7%	Sodium	656mg

THAI NOODLE SALAD

Makes 4 servings

Lime juice and chile in the dressing makes it a Thai-style salad; rice vinegar and nori seaweed make it Japanese-style (see Variation).

Cook the pasta according to package directions until tender. Meanwhile, prepare the vegetables (and tofu, if using). Blend all of the dressing ingredients in a blender or food processor. Drain the pasta and place in a serving bowl with the dressing and other ingredients, except sesame seeds. Toss well. Sprinkle with the sesame seeds. Serve at room temperature.

For **JAPANESE-STYLE SALAD**, omit the mint, basil, or cilantro and substitute ½ cup shredded toasted nori seaweed (the kind you use for sushi rolls). For the dressing, use rice vinegar instead of lime juice, and omit the jalapeño.

PER SERVING:			
Calories	286	FIBER	5g
Total Fat	4g	Carbohydrate	52g
Saturated Fat	1g	Protein	12g
Calories from fat	12%	Sodium	1515mg

SALAD

½ lb. whole grain vermicelli pasta or udon noodles

½ English (seedless) cucumber, sliced into thin strips

1 large red bell pepper, seeded and cut into strips

¼ cup chopped fresh mint, basil, or cilantro

OPTIONAL

2 cups thinly sliced strips grilled portobello or cremini mushrooms OR commercial marinated savory baked tofu

DRESSING

¼ cup light soy sauce

3 tablespoons lime juice

2 tablespoons sugar or alternate

1 tablespoon chopped fresh ginger

1 tablespoon pickled jalapeño pepper

1 clove garlic, peeled

2 tablespoons toasted sesame seeds for garnish

CHINESE VEGETABLE-NOODLE SALAD

with Sesame

Makes 8 servings

This is a very easy, versatile, and delicious salad, adapted from a recipe in Deborah Madison's Vegetarian Cooking for Everyone *(Broadway Books, NY, 1997). I take it to potlucks frequently and invariably have several requests for the recipe. You can substitute other vegetables if you don't have the ones I suggest.*

Cook the pasta according to package directions until tender; drain well. Mix the Dressing ingredients well and pour over the noodles; toss well. Add the green onions, sesame seeds, vegetables, red bell pepper and tofu, if using. Toss again. Store in the refrigerator, but bring to room temperature before serving.

1 pound whole grain spaghettini or soba noodles

2 bunches green onions, chopped

¼ cup toasted sesame seeds or chopped roasted peanuts

1 pound lightly cooked whole green beans or asparagus, cut into 2-inch lengths OR broccoli flowerettes, thinly sliced

1 red bell pepper, sliced (optional)

Baked, flavored tofu, thinly sliced (optional)

DRESSING

7 tablespoons light soy sauce

¼ cup toasted sesame oil

3½ tablespoons brown sugar

3 tablespoons balsamic vinegar

3 tablespoons water

1 tablespoon grated fresh ginger

2 teaspoons salt

1 teaspoon Chinese chili garlic paste

1-2 cloves garlic, crushed

PER SERVING:			
Calories	358	FIBER	10.6g
Total Fat	10g	Carbohydrate	59g
Saturated Fat	1g	Protein	13g
Calories from fat	25%	Sodium	1156mg

THAI CABBAGE SALAD

Makes 4 servings

This slaw makes a great winter accompaniment to an Asian meal.

Mix all of the salad ingredients in a serving bowl. Combine all of the dressing ingredients in a small bowl. Add dressing to salad; toss well. Refrigerate until serving time.

3 cups finely shredded
fresh green cabbage

1 medium carrot, shredded

1 small sweet onion, thinly sliced

2 tablespoons minced
fresh cilantro or parsley

2 tablespoons minced fresh mint
or 2 teaspoons dried mint

DRESSING

2 tablespoons light soy sauce

2 tablespoons lime or lemon juice

2 tablespoons water or
light vegetable broth

1 tablespoon sugar or alternative

1 tablespoon slivered lime or lemon zest

PER SERVING:			
Calories	55	FIBER	2.3g
Total Fat	0g	Carbohydrate	12g
Saturated Fat	0g	Protein	2g
Calories from fat	0%	Sodium	365mg

Quick Tip

Crisp greens and lettuce

As soon as you pick the greens or bring them home from the market, separate the leaves, discard any bad ones, and soak them in cold water for 15 minutes. Dry the leaves in a salad spinner, or lay the leaves on a large clean towel, roll the towel up loosely, then spin the towel around, holding tightly to both ends. An old-fashioned way of drying salad greens without bruising them is to place them in an old but clean pillow case (actually, using two pillowcases, one inside the other, provides more absorption capacity), stand outside, and whirl it around like mad!

Remove the leaves, wrap them in moist clean tea towels, and place them in plastic bags (there are specially-made ones available now that keep vegetables fresh longer—look for them in the vegetable section of your market) or special plastic salad storage containers. Store in the refrigerator. Lettuce and other greens will keep crisp and fresh longer if you take a few minutes to do this, and they will be ready at a moment's notice. This method can also be used to revive wilted lettuce.

TABBOULEH
(Bulghur and Parsley Salad)

Makes 8 to 12 servings

This popular Middle Eastern salad has long been a staple for vegetarians, but it usually contains way too much olive oil. My version contains far less oil, but none of the flavor is missing. Tabbouleh should be vibrant and flavorful. A Lebanese friend told me that an authentic tabbouleh must have lots of parsley—it should be very green. Italian parsley is the tastiest, but you can use ordinary parsley or a combination. Fresh mint and dill add a delightful fresh flavor. The traditional (and very attractive) way to serve tabbouleh is to mound it in a serving bowl or platter with a rim and surround it with crisp romaine lettuce leaves to use as scoopers. Decorate the salad with tomato wedges, sprigs of fresh mint and parsley, and black kalamata olives.

PER SERVING: with garnish			
Calories	119	FIBER	4.2g
Total Fat	7g	Carbohydrate	15g
Saturated Fat	1g	Protein	3g
Calories from fat	52%	Sodium	283mg

SALAD
1 cup dry bulghur

1 cup boiling water

4 cups minced fresh parsley

2 ripe, firm tomatoes, diced

½ large English (seedless) cucumber, diced

½ cup chopped fresh mint

½ cup chopped green onion

3 tablespoons fresh, chopped dill weed or 1 tablespoon dried dill weed

½ large green bell pepper, seeded and chopped (optional)

DRESSING
½ cup No-Fat Oil Substitute (p. 67)

¼ cup extra-virgin olive oil*

¼ cup fresh lemon juice

1 teaspoon salt

Pepper to taste

GARNISH
2 heads romaine lettuce

2 firm, ripe tomatoes, cut into wedges

Sprigs parsley and mint

12 kalamata olives

To make the salad, mix the bulghur and boiling water in a large serving bowl; let stand while you prepare the vegetables and dressing.

To make the dressing, whisk all of the ingredients together; chill.

When the bulghur has absorbed all of the water, add all of the remaining salad ingredients and the dressing. Toss well. Season to taste with salt and pepper; refrigerate.

To serve, mound tabbouleh in a serving bowl or a platter with a rim, and surround it with crisp romaine lettuce leaves to use as scoopers. Decorate the salad with tomato wedges, sprigs of fresh parsley and mint, and kalamata olives.

TIP: Mince fresh parsley in a food processor. Make sure it is completely dry, so that it doesn't clump together or become puréed.

*TO REDUCE FAT AND CALORIES, use one of the no-fat oil substitutes on page 67 for up to ¼ cup of the olive oil—I usually use chickpea cooking broth—but use at least 1 tablespoon of olive oil.

COUSCOUS TABBOULEH: Use cooked whole wheat couscous or RizCous instead of bulghur.

QUINOA TABBOULEH: Use cooked quinoa instead of bulghur.

SPROUTED WHEAT TABBOULEH: If you are a sprout fan, add a handful or two of sprouted wheat (with the sprout no longer than the wheat kernel itself), well-drained and coarsely chopped.

FULL-MEAL TABBOULEH: This isn't traditional, but it's delicious anyway! Add 2 cups cooked or canned rinsed and well-drained chickpeas or lentils. You may need a little more dressing for this because there will be a larger volume with the addition of the legumes.

GRILLED VEGETABLE TABBOULEH: Omit the cucumber, tomatoes, and green pepper, and layer the tabbouleh with cold grilled vegetables. Top the salad with chickpeas that have marinated in a vinaigrette dressing.

"USE YOUR IMAGINATION" TABBOULEH: Once you get the hang of making tabbouleh, you can let your imagination run free! Add some chopped toasted walnuts or pecans (and use nut oil instead of some of the olive oil, perhaps). Use some fresh orange juice in place of the broth in the dressing and add chopped orange to the salad. Add some chopped celery, marinated artichoke hearts, oil-packed sun-dried tomatoes, roasted red bell peppers...

Fruity Brown Basmati Salad

Makes 6 to 8 servings

This is a lovely, virtually fat-free salad—great for potlucks.

Cook the rice in the boiling water with the salt and sesame oil, covered, over low heat, 45 minutes, or until dry and fluffy.

Mix the cooked rice in a bowl with all of the dressing ingredients; toss, and let stand 15 minutes. Add all of the veggies and nuts; toss again. Serve immediately or refrigerate.

RICE

1 cup raw brown basmati rice

1½ cups boiling water

1 teaspoon toasted sesame oil

¼ teaspoon salt

DRESSING

¼ cup orange juice (preferably freshly squeezed)

2 tablespoons soy sauce

1½ tablespoons maple syrup

2 tablespoons cider, rice, or white wine vinegar

8 ounces canned crushed unsweetened pineapple, drained

VEGGIES, ETC.

2-3 green onions, chopped

2-3 stalks celery or fennel bulb, chopped

½ cup pea, sunflower, or broccoli sprouts

½ cup raisins or other dried fruit (cranberries or blueberries are good)

1 cup frozen baby peas, thawed

¼ cup roasted nuts or seeds

1 small green bell pepper, seeded and chopped

1 small red bell pepper, seeded and chopped

PER SERVING:			
Calories	197	FIBER	4.4g
Total Fat	4g	Carbohydrate	37g
Saturated Fat	1g	Protein	5g
Calories from fat	18%	Sodium	385mg

Persian Potato and Pickle Salad
(Salad-e Khiar Shur)

Makes 8 servings

This colorful salad is perfect for any holiday buffet.

Assemble all of the salad ingredients in a large bowl. To make the dressing, place the broth and starch in a small saucepan and stir over high heat until it thickens and turns clear (cornstarch has to boil; potato starch does not). Whisk or blend in all of the remaining dressing ingredients and pour over the salad. Toss well. Taste for salt. Refrigerate at least 1 hour or overnight.

VARIATIONS

1) Substitute pickled carrots for regular carrots.

2) If you like to use some oil, use only ½ cup of the starch mixture or chickpea broth, and ¼ cup extra-virgin olive oil.

3) If you prefer a creamy dressing, add ½ cup low-fat mayonnaise and blend the dressing well in a blender until creamy and smooth.

SALAD

4 medium carrots, cooked and diced

1½-2 cups cooked or canned red kidney beans or small red beans, drained

2 large cooked, unpeeled red-skinned potatoes, diced

2 large dill pickles, chopped

10 radishes, sliced

1 bunch green onions, chopped

1 bunch parsley, minced

¼ cup chopped fresh mint or 2 tablespoons dried

½ small head green cabbage, cored and shredded (optional)

DRESSING

¾ cup cold vegetable broth

2 teaspoons cornstarch

½ cup lemon juice

1 to 2 cloves garlic, crushed

1 teaspoon salt

1 teaspoon dried tarragon

½ teaspoon white pepper

PER SERVING:			
Calories	109	FIBER	4.9g
Total Fat	0g	Carbohydrate	23g
Saturated Fat	0g	Protein	5g
Calories from fat	0%	Sodium	496mg

FATTOUSH
(Lebanese Pita Bread and Tomato Salad with Herbs)

Makes 6 servings

The seasonings of this salad will remind you of Tabbouleh (page 76); however it is distinctly different and uniquely delicious! While it was originally invented, no doubt, as a way to use up stale pita bread, you can toast fresh pita bread for the same effect (sort of like making croutons).

In Lebanon, you might find the herbs purslane and sumac in this salad, as well as pungent greens that are unfamiliar to us. In Lebanese restaurants in North America, Fattoush is usually made simply with mint, parsley, and perhaps watercress—and it's always scrumptious!

To make the dressing, mix all of the dressing ingredients together in a blender, with a whisk, or shake them in a tightly sealed jar.

Just before serving, place the lettuce in a large bowl. Add all of the remaining salad ingredients. Add the dressing; toss well. Divide the salad among 6 plates, and serve immediately.

DRESSING

¼ cup extra-virgin olive oil

¼ cup vegetable broth

⅓ cup fresh lemon juice

1-2 cloves garlic, crushed

Salt and freshly ground pepper to taste

2 teaspoons ground sumac (optional)

SALAD

1 head romaine lettuce, torn into bite-size pieces

1 medium English (seedless) cucumber, diced

4 green onions, chopped

½ cup chopped fresh parsley (Italian or flat-leaf, if possible)

¼ cup chopped fresh mint

1 large whole wheat pita bread (or 2 small ones), split, toasted, and torn into bite-size pieces

OPTIONAL

1 green bell pepper, seeded and chopped

1 cup chopped purslane

½-1 cup torn arugula or watercress leaves or a mixture

PER SERVING:

Calories	146	FIBER	3g
Total Fat	10g	Carbohydrate	14g
Saturated Fat	1g	Protein	3g
Calories from fat	61%	Sodium	88mg

LEE'S BLACK-EYED PEA SALAD

Makes 6 servings

My good friend Lee Hoffman of New Orleans gave me the original recipe for this salad. It is colorful, delicious, and full of nutrition.

Mix all of the ingredients in a medium salad bowl or decorative serving bowl. Refrigerate until serving time (it will keep for several days, refrigerated). Stir again before serving. Serve it "as is," on a bed of crisp lettuce or baby spinach leaves, or wrapped in a flour tortilla.

1 (10-12 ounce) bag or box frozen black-eyed peas, cooked and drained, or 2 cups cooked or canned black-eyed peas, drained

¾ cup chopped red bell pepper

¾ cup grated green cabbage

¾ cup Italian Wine Vinegar Dressing (p. 66)

1 carrot, grated

4 green onions, chopped

Pinch of cayenne pepper

PER SERVING:			
Calories	320	FIBER	4.8g
Total Fat	27g	Carbohydrate	16g
Saturated Fat	4g	Protein	5g
Calories from fat	75%	Sodium	224mg

CHICKPEA AND WALNUT SALAD
with Lemon Dressing

Makes 6 servings

Serve this mixture inside edible wrappers of crisp romaine lettuce.

Mash the chickpeas in a small serving bowl with the back of a fork. Add the walnuts. Whisk together the lemon juice, oil, garlic, and salt in a small bowl. Combine the dressing with the chickpea-walnut mixture. Chill. Just before serving, fill leaves with a heaping spoonful of salad and arrange on a platter. Serve immediately.

1 (15-ounce) can chickpeas or 1½ cup cooked chickpeas, drained

⅔ cup minced toasted walnuts

6 tablespoons fresh lemon juice

¼ cup extra-virgin olive oil or No-Fat Oil Substitute (p. 67)

2 cloves garlic, crushed

½ teaspoon salt or to taste

2 heads crisp romaine lettuce leaves

PER SERVING:			
Calories	242	FIBER	3.6g
Total Fat	18g	Carbohydrate	16g
Saturated Fat	2g	Protein	6g
Calories from fat	66%	Sodium	185mg

FRENCH POTATO AND GREEN BEAN SALAD

Makes 8-12 servings

In a large saucepan, cover the potatoes with water and bring to a boil. Cover and simmer until tender but firm. Drain in a colander and peel them with your fingers under running cold water. Drain again and cut into medium dice or thick slices, as desired. Toss the potatoes in a serving bowl with the wine, green onion, tarragon, and salt and pepper. Set aside.

Cook the green beans in boiling water to cover about 5 minutes or until crisp-tender. Drain and cool under cold running water. Drain again. Fold the green beans into the potato mixture.

To make the vinaigrette, place the broth and starch in a small saucepan and stir over high heat until it thickens and turns clear. (Cornstarch has to boil; potato starch does not.) Whisk or blend in the vinegar and salt. Pour the hot mixture over the potatoes and beans and stir gently, sprinkling with pepper to taste.

Refrigerate the salad until ready to serve. Toss the salad gently and taste for salt. Arrange the tomato wedges decoratively on top and serve cold or at room temperature on crisp romaine lettuce leaves, if you like.

4 pounds new boiling potatoes or red-skinned potatoes, unpeeled (cut into uniform chunks)

¼ cup dry white wine, or rice, cider, or white wine vinegar

¼ cup minced green onion

¼ cup minced fresh tarragon or basil

Salt and freshly ground pepper to taste

1 pound fresh green beans, ends trimmed, cut into 2-inch pieces or frozen whole small green beans, snapped in half

Freshly ground pepper to taste

4 small ripe, firm tomatoes, cut in wedges

Romaine leaves

VINAIGRETTE

¾ cup cold vegetable broth*

2 teaspoons cornstarch or potato starch

⅓ cup white wine vinegar, or rice or cider vinegar

1-1½ teaspoons salt

*NOTE: If you prefer not to use the starch mixture, use broth from cooking chickpeas. If you like to use some oil, use only ½ cup of the starch mixture or chickpea broth, and ¼ cup extra-virgin olive oil.

PER SERVING:			
Calories	194	FIBER	5.8g
Total Fat	0g	Carbohydrate	44g
Saturated Fat	0g	Protein	5g
Calories from fat	0%	Sodium	283mg

CHRISTMAS CRANBERRY SALAD
with Baby Spinach and Pecans

Makes 6 servings

I got the idea for this salad for my vegan Christmas buffet from a picture out of an old "Better Homes and Gardens" magazine (the recipe was missing). It was delicious and a big hit! Salads often remain behind at Christmas dinners, but this one was gobbled up fast! There's lots of room for experimentation.

2 cups fresh cranberries

½ cup water

¼ cup sugar or maple syrup

6 cups baby spinach

3 large oranges, peeled and thinly sliced

8-ounce fennel bulb, cut into thin strips

¾ cup chopped toasted pecans or other nuts

½ cup Balsamic Vinaigrette (p. 68), made with optional sugar or maple syrup

Well ahead of serving time, combine the cranberries, water, and sugar. Bring to a boil, then boil gently, covered, 2 minutes. Pour into a bowl, cover, and chill. Drain the cranberries, reserving 1 tablespoon of syrup.

Arrange the spinach on 6 salad plates or on a large platter. Arrange the oranges, fennel, cranberries, and nuts on top. Mix the reserved 1 tablespoon cranberry syrup with the dressing and drizzle over the salad. Serve immediately.

VARIATIONS

1) Substitute other berries, such as raspberries, for the cranberries.

2) Use an aromatic nut oil in the vinaigrette.

3) Substitute another crunchy vegetable for the fennel bulb: jicama, Jerusalem artichoke, or celery.

PER SERVING:			
Calories	227	FIBER	6.1g
Total Fat	13g	Carbohydrate	28g
Saturated Fat	1g	Protein	4g
Calories from fat	51%	Sodium	256mg

DAIRY-FREE BECHAMEL

makes 2 cups (8 servings)

This rich-tasting sauce is actually quite low in fat. It can be used as an all-purpose white sauce in all of your cooking, and as a topping for Greek dishes, such as vegetarian moussaka, and even as a substitute for melted cheese in many casseroles. In Italy, this type of sauce is used on lasagne rather than the heavy melted cheeses in American-style lasagne.

Place all of the Blended Mixture ingredients, EXCEPT the nutmeg and pepper, in the blender and blend until VERY smooth. Set aside.

Melt the margarine in a medium, heavy saucepan and whisk in the flour. Whisk it over medium-high heat for a few minutes, but remove from heat before it starts to change color (you want a white "roux"). Scrape this into the Blended Mixture and blend for a few seconds, then pour the mixture back into the pot. Stir over medium-high heat until it thickens and boils; turn down and simmer on low for a few minutes. Whisk in the nutmeg and pepper.

2 tablespoons dairy-free margarine or extra-virgin olive oil

1½ to 3 tablespoons unbleached flour (depending on thickness desired)

BLENDED MIXTURE

1 cup nondairy milk

½ cup extra-firm SILKEN tofu or regular medium-firm tofu, crumbled

½ cup water

1 "chicken-style" vegetarian broth cube (or enough for 1 cup of liquid), crumbled

½ teaspoon salt

a large pinch EACH of freshly grated nutmeg and white pepper

PER SERVING:			
Calories	52	FIBER	.6g
Total Fat	4g	Carbohydrate	2g
Saturated Fat	1g	Protein	4g
Calories from fat	69%	Sodium	149mg

SOUPS

You may be surprised to find such a large chapter on soups in a fiber cookbook, but soups are one of the most delicious ways to add fiber to your diet. Personally, I can eat soup for any meal—including breakfast and snacks—and frequently do so. They are cheap, filling, and versatile. Every culture has soup, so you could eat a different soup just about every day of your life and never get through all the possibilities!

For people who claim to dislike vegetables, grains, and/or beans, soups are the perfect way to consume these foods. It's not that they're disguised exactly, but they are not just confronting you on a plate, so to speak! They are mixed with other foods in a tasty broth, perhaps even puréed. You can purée beans, potatoes, or grains to make soups creamy without the cream. You can add some cooked beans and grains to vegetable soup to make it a meal. Leftovers make excellent soup material, too.

If you're not used to making your own soups, it will come as a nice surprise to learn how easy it is. I like to have some homemade soup in my refrigerator or freezer at all times for quick, homey meals, or for a low-fat, filling snack.

CREAMY VEGETABLE SOUP

Makes 4 servings

A very simple concept—simmer potatoes and whatever other vegetables you like in broth, then purée it for a thick and creamy soup—hot or cold, without fat or dairy!

In an oiled nonstick medium pot over high heat, stir-fry the onion and garlic for 5 minutes, adding a splash of water as needed to keep from sticking. Do not brown. Add the vegetables, potatoes, broth, salt, and optional seasonings except lemon juice. Bring to a boil, cover, reduce heat, and simmer 10-15 minutes or until vegetables and potatoes are tender. Purée cooked vegetables in the pot with a hand immersion blender or transfer vegetables to the food processor or blender with a slotted spoon; purée, leaving an opening in the lid for steam to escape to prevent an explosion. Cover the opening loosely with a folded cloth as you purée. Add a bit of the broth, then stir the puréed mixture back into the pot. Taste for salt and pepper. Add lemon juice, if using. Serve with 1 or 2 of the garnishes.

1 medium onion, chopped

1 clove garlic, minced

2 stalks celery, chopped (optional)

1 pound vegetables, chopped (see possibilities on facing page)

2 medium russet potatoes (about ½ pound), peeled and diced

3 cups vegetable broth

½ teaspoon salt

Pepper to taste

OPTIONAL ADDITIONS

1 tablespoon curry powder

2 teaspoons powdered ginger

¼ teaspoon nutmeg

Pinch of cayenne

1-3 teaspoons lemon juice

GARNISHES

Plain soy yogurt, nondairy sour cream

Extra-virgin olive oil for drizzling

Minced fresh parsley, mint, basil, dill weed, or cilantro

Paprika, curry powder, croutons, chopped green onions or chives, etc.

PER SERVING:			
Calories	117	FIBER	4.6g
Total Fat	1g	Carbohydrate	26g
Saturated Fat	0g	Protein	4g
Calories from fat	7%	Sodium	314mg

Vegetable Possibilities for Creamy Vegetable Soup

Carrots, zucchini,
or other summer squash

Pumpkin (14-ounce can),
or other winter squash

Sweet potato (perhaps with
an apple added)

Leafy greens (10-ounce chopped frozen),
cauliflower, broccoli, asparagus, leeks

Roasted, sautéed, or grilled yellow,
orange, or red bell peppers

Fresh shelled peas or frozen baby peas

Parsnip, yellow turnip, or rutabaga
(perhaps add a carrot)

GAZPACHO

Makes 4-6 servings

*The addition of canned black beans
gives color as well as fiber.*

Combine all of the ingredients in a serving bowl or pitcher, and serve immediately, or refrigerate.

½ medium English (seedless)
cucumber, chopped

1 medium ripe, firm tomato,
trimmed and chopped

1 small onion, peeled and minced

½ large green bell pepper,
seeded and chopped

1 clove garlic, crushed

3 cups chilled tomato juice
or vegetable cocktail

1 (15-ounce) can or 1½ cups
cooked black beans or black soybeans,
rinsed and drained (optional)

2 tablespoons red wine, balsamic vinegar,
fresh lemon juice, or fresh lime juice

1 tablespoon minced
fresh parsley or basil

½ teaspoon sugar or alternative

½ teaspoon salt

½ teaspoon vegetarian Worcestershire
sauce (optional)

Whole grain croutons (optional)

PER SERVING:			
Calories	126	FIBER	6.6g
Total Fat	1g	Carbohydrate	25g
Saturated Fat	0g	Protein	7g
Calories from fat	7%	Sodium	744mg

Classic Mushroom and Barley Soup

Makes 6-8 servings

This is a very rich-tasting soup, great on a cold day. It's one of my absolute favorites. This version is a typical Eastern European variety, but I have added a few cooked beans for extra fiber and protein.

Soak the dried mushrooms in boiling water to cover for 30 minutes. Meanwhile, heat the olive oil in a soup pot. Add the onion, celery, 2 tablespoons of the parsley, carrots, garlic, and fresh mushrooms, and sauté about 5 minutes. Stir in the flour. Slowly add the broth.

Drain the dried mushrooms, reserving the liquid. Chop the mushrooms and add them to the pot along with the reserved liquid, barley, and yeast extract. Add the beans. Bring to a boil, then reduce heat, cover, and simmer 1 hour. Taste for salt and pepper.

If the soup is too thick, add more broth until desired consistency is reached.

½ ounce dried boletus or porcini mushrooms

2 tablespoons olive oil

1 large onion, thinly sliced

2 stalks celery with leaves, chopped

¼ cup parsley, chopped

2 carrots, diced

3-4 cloves garlic, chopped

1 pound sliced fresh cremini, portobello, or chanterelle mushrooms

1 tablespoon wheat or rice flour

8 cups vegetable broth

1-2 teaspoons Marmite, Vegemite or other yeast extract or 2-4 teaspoons dark or red miso

1 cup Scotch or pot barley

1 cup cooked or canned soybeans or black-eyed peas, rinsed and drained

Salt and pepper to taste

PER SERVING:			
Calories	216	FIBER	6.7g
Total Fat	7g	Carbohydrate	35g
Saturated Fat	1g	Protein	8g
Calories from fat	29%	Sodium	99mg

ZUCCHINI BISQUE

Makes 6 servings

This is absolutely scrumptious and uses up 2½ pounds of zucchini—a boon for summer zucchini bounty time! With their peels intact, zucchini and other summer squash contain a respectable amount of dietary fiber. Since this soup is essentially puréed zucchini, it's a delicious way to get some fiber.

2-3 tablespoons extra-virgin olive oil

2½ pounds zucchini or other summer squash, unpeeled, cubed

4 cloves garlic, minced

2¾ cup vegetable broth

¼ cup nondairy milk blended with 2 tablespoons chopped raw cashews

Salt and freshly ground pepper to taste

Soy Parmesan

Heat the olive oil in a medium pot. Add the zucchini and garlic and sauté over medium heat 10 minutes. Do not brown zucchini.

Add the broth and simmer 5-10 minutes. Transfer ⅔ of the soup to a food processor or blender; purée, leaving an opening in the lid for steam to escape to prevent an explosion. Cover the opening loosely with a folded cloth as you purée. Or, blend coarsely with a hand immersion blender in the pot.

Purée the milk and cashews in a blender, or blend coarsely with an immersion blender right in the pot. Add to soup, and taste for salt and pepper. Heat briefly. Serve with soy Parmesan.

PER SERVING:			
Calories	97	FIBER	2.5g
Total Fat	8g	Carbohydrate	7g
Saturated Fat	1g	Protein	3g
Calories from fat	74%	Sodium	7mg

ITALIAN WINTER SQUASH AND SWEET POTATO SOUP

Makes 6-8 servings

In North America, we are used to winter squash cooked with maple syrup or brown sugar. The pairing of sweet squash with savory broth and cheese takes some getting used to for some people, but it is delightful. This soup is perfect for a cold winter day.

A "meaty" squash such as butternut or the blue-gray hubbard type, combined with orange sweet potato, is the closest we can get to the Italian pumpkin or "zucca" that is traditional in this soup. If you cook the squash and sweet potato in a pressure cooker, this soup is very quick to make.

1 medium butternut or hubbard squash

2 large (about 6-inch) sweet potatoes

2 tablespoons nondairy margarine

2 medium onions, sliced

6-7 cups vegetable broth

Salt and freshly ground pepper to taste

Pinch of freshly ground nutmeg

4 slices whole grain Italian bread, crusts removed

Soy Parmesan

Cut the squash in half with a cleaver or large knife. Scrape out the seeds and discard. Cut the squash into eighths. Cut the sweet potatoes into about 6 equal pieces each.

TO PRESSURE-COOK: The squash and sweet potatoes can be cooked together in the steam-basket for 6 minutes at high pressure (15 pounds). Release pressure under running water. When cool enough to handle, peel off the sweet potato skins and discard, and scoop the soft flesh out of the squash skins.

MICROWAVE OPTION: Place the squash pieces in a large microwave casserole, add about ¼ cup water, cover, and cook on HIGH for about 10 minutes. Scoop the soft flesh out of the peel and set aside. Peel the sweet potato and cut into 1-inch pieces. Place in a glass pie plate with 2 tablespoons water, cover, and cook on HIGH about 5 minutes.

Melt the margarine in a heavy soup pot. Add the onions and sauté over medium heat until onions are soft and translucent.

PER SERVING:			
Calories	169	FIBER	4.9g
Total Fat	4g	Carbohydrate	31g
Saturated Fat	1g	Protein	4g
Calories from fat	21%	Sodium	177mg

Do not brown. Add a little bit of water to prevent sticking. Add the cooked squash and sweet potato and the broth and bring to a boil. Reduce heat to a simmer, cover, and simmer 5 minutes.

Blend the soup in the pot with a hand immersion blender or transfer to a food processor or blender with a slotted spoon. Blend, leaving an opening in the lid for steam to escape to prevent an explosion. Cover the opening loosely with a folded cloth as you purée. The soup should have some texture and not be completely puréed. Pour it back into the pot and keep it warm over low heat while you taste for salt and pepper and add a pinch of nutmeg.

Toast the bread and cut it into ½-inch cubes. Serve the soup with a sprinkling of the croutons and some soy Parmesan.

VEGETABLE OATMEAL SOUP

Makes 6-8 servings

Oatmeal in soup?! Trust me, it's delicious! This is quick and simple, and contains no exotic ingredients. I wouldn't hesitate to serve it to company with some nice, fresh bread.

2 tablespoons extra-virgin olive oil

2 cups thinly sliced carrots

1 large onion, chopped

1 cup chopped celery

2 cloves garlic, minced

1 cup rolled oats

8 cups vegetable broth

1 cup canned or fresh diced tomatoes

1 teaspoon dried thyme

1 cup frozen baby peas

Salt and freshly ground pepper to taste

In a large heavy pot, heat the oil over medium-high heat. Add the carrots, onion, celery, and garlic. When the onion starts to soften, add the oats and stir-fry 2-3 minutes. Add the broth, tomatoes, thyme, and peas, bring to a boil, reduce heat, cover, and simmer about 15 minutes. Taste for salt and pepper.

PER SERVING:			
Calories	127	FIBER	4.2g
Total Fat	5g	Carbohydrate	18g
Saturated Fat	1g	Protein	4g
Calories from fat	35%	Sodium	84mg

DAL RASAM
(Southern Indian Thin Spicy Soup or "Pepper Water")

Makes 6 servings

Rasam is said to aid digestion and is served either as a second course or throughout the meal. Tamarind water (or lemon juice) lends a typically tangy South Indian flavor, and a baghar or chaunk (spice mixture) is employed here to add rich flavor. I use olive or peanut oil in place of ghee (Indian clarified butter). Rasam makes a good light lunch with some plain rice and a salad.

In a medium pot, bring the split peas and water to a boil, then reduce heat, cover and cook until tender, 25-45 minutes. Add the tomatoes, tamarind water, garlic, salt, cumin, black pepper, and chilies. Simmer about 15 minutes more.

Meanwhile, heat the oil in a small heavy skillet over high heat. Add the mustard seeds and bay leaves and stir constantly until the mustard seeds start to pop. Remove from the heat and pour over the soup. Taste for salt and serve hot by itself or over plain rice.

¼ cup split yellow peas, or red or green lentils

4 cups water

2 medium ripe tomatoes, chopped, or about 1½ cups canned diced tomatoes

1 cup hot water mixed with 1 tablespoon tamarind paste OR 1 cup fresh lemon juice

4 cloves garlic, minced

2 teaspoons salt

1 teaspoon ground cumin

¾ teaspoon freshly ground pepper

1-2 dried red chiles, crumbled

Cooked rice (optional)

BAGHAR (SPICE MIXTURE)

¼ cup olive oil or expeller-pressed Chinese peanut oil

1 teaspoon black or yellow mustard seeds

4 bay leaves or curry leaves, crumbled

PER SERVING:			
Calories	140	FIBER	3.4g
Total Fat	9g	Carbohydrate	13g
Saturated Fat	1g	Protein	3g
Calories from fat	50%	Sodium	715mg

SICILIAN-STYLE SPLIT PEA SOUP

Makes 6 servings

This thick, spicy soup—which is unlike any other split-pea soup you've ever tasted, I guarantee—was a favorite when my children were young.

Heat the olive oil in a large heavy pot. Add the onion, carrots, celery, and garlic, and sauté until the onions have softened. Add broth, split peas, tomatoes, herbs, and spices, and bring to a boil. Cover, reduce heat, and simmer about 1½ hours or until the peas are soft.

Meanwhile, cook the pasta in boiling salted water until almost done. Drain and add to the soup when the peas are soft. Taste for salt and stir in the sesame oil. Serve hot.

2 tablespoons extra-virgin olive oil

1 large onion, chopped

2 carrots, chopped

2 stalks celery, chopped

3 cloves garlic, minced

5 cups vegetable broth

1 cup dried split peas

1 (28-ounce) can diced tomatoes

¼ cup chopped fresh Italian parsley

1 bay leaf

1 small dried red hot chile, crumbled

¼ teaspoon each dried thyme, basil, and freshly ground black pepper

3-4 ounces whole grain macaroni

Salt to taste

1 teaspoon toasted sesame oil

PER SERVING:			
Calories	246	FIBER	11.1g
Total Fat	6g	Carbohydrate	40g
Saturated Fat	1g	Protein	11g
Calories from fat	21%	Sodium	241mg

LENTIL SOUP, MY WAY

Makes 8 servings

Lentil soup has been one of my favorites since childhood—my mother used to make her version several times a month, and we never tired of it. I like to add a little red wine, some herbs, and quinoa— a high-protein whole grain from Peru—making a very hearty soup that needs only crusty bread and perhaps a salad to make a meal.

In a large soup pot with a heavy bottom, heat the olive oil over medium-high heat. Add the onions and sauté until they begin to soften. Add the carrots (if using), celery, and garlic, and sauté a few minutes more. Add the broth, lentils, tomatoes, red wine, and herbs. Bring to a boil, reduce heat, and simmer, covered, for about 1½ hours. Taste for salt and pepper, and add bouillon cubes for flavor if necessary. Add the quinoa and the greens (if using), and cook 15 minutes more. Garnish with sesame oil and soy Parmesan, if you like.

PER SERVING:			
Calories	209	FIBER	10.3g
Total Fat	4g	Carbohydrate	31g
Saturated Fat	1g	Protein	11g
Calories from fat	17%	Sodium	205mg

2 tablespoons extra-virgin olive oil

2 medium onions, chopped

2 carrots, chopped (optional)

2 stalks celery, chopped

2 cloves garlic, minced

8 cups light vegetable broth or water

1½ cups dried brown lentils

1 (28-ounce) can diced tomatoes

½ cup dry red wine

2 bay leaves

½ teaspoon each dried basil and thyme

Salt and pepper to taste

1-2 vegetarian bouillon cubes (optional)

½ cup uncooked quinoa, rinsed and drained

Salt and freshly ground pepper to taste

1 cup chopped cooked greens or 1 (10-ounce) package frozen chopped spinach, thawed and squeezed dry (optional)

Toasted sesame oil and soy Parmesan cheese for garnish

VARIATION

LENTIL STEW: Use only 6 cups broth or water and 2 cups lentils. Use the carrots and omit the quinoa and greens. This can be served with vegetarian "Italian sausage," browned, or cooked vegetarian weiners.

Vegetarian Mulligatawny

Makes 6 servings

"Mulligatawny" is an Anglicized Indian word that roughly translates to "pepper water." It is usually made with chicken, but this meatless version is hearty and satisfying.

Stir-fry the onions, celery, carrot, and garlic in an oiled medium soup pot over medium-high heat about 5 minutes, adding a few drops of water as necessary to keep from sticking. When the onions have softened, add the peppers and curry powder and stir-fry for 3 minutes. Add the remaining ingredients, bring to a boil, then reduce heat, cover, and simmer 15 minutes. Taste for salt and pepper and serve.

2 large onions, chopped

2 stalks celery, chopped

1 carrot, chopped

2-3 cloves garlic, minced

1 red bell pepper, seeded and finely diced

1 green bell pepper, seeded and finely diced

1 teaspoon curry powder or garam masala

5 cups vegetable broth

2 cups cooked brown rice

1 (15-ounce) can or 1½ cups cooked black-eyed peas, drained and coarsely mashed

½ small can (6 tablespoons) tomato paste

2 tablespoons minced fresh parsley

Salt and pepper to taste

PER SERVING:

Calories	170	FIBER	6.9g
Total Fat	1g	Carbohydrate	34g
Saturated Fat	0g	Protein	7g
Calories from fat	5%	Sodium	61mg

Velvet Turkish Red Lentil Soup

Makes 6 servings

I had a red lentil soup in a Turkish restaurant called "Istanbul," in Calgary, where my friend Val Fitch took me to see some bellydancing. This soup is very common in Turkey, and there are myriad variations. My cousin Chris Tonge, who claims not to care for legumes, absolutely raves about it.

1 tablespoon extra-virgin olive oil

2 small onions, chopped

2 tablespoons flour

4 cups vegetable broth

⅔ cup split red lentils, rinsed

¾ cup rich nondairy milk or organic nondairy creamer, mixed with 1½ tablespoons cornstarch

¼ teaspoon salt, or more if broth is unsalted

Freshly ground pepper to taste

2 thick slices whole grain bread

In a medium-sized heavy pot, heat the oil over medium-high heat. Add the onion and sauté for a few minutes. Stir in the flour, blending it well. Add the broth gradually, stirring constantly. Add the lentils. Simmer about 30 minutes, uncovered, or until the lentils are tender.

Purée the soup in the pot with a hand immersion blender or transfer to a food processor or blender with a slotted spoon; purée, leaving an opening in the lid for steam to escape to prevent an explosion. Cover the opening loosely with a folded cloth as you purée.

Stir in the cornstarch mixture, and simmer gently 2 minutes. Add salt and pepper to taste. Toast the bread and cut it into small cubes. Serve the soup hot with the bread cubes.

PER SERVING:			
Calories	126	FIBER	5.5g
Total Fat	4g	Carbohydrate	18g
Saturated Fat	1g	Protein	7g
Calories from fat	28%	Sodium	129mg

HABITANT PEA SOUP

Makes 6-8 servings

"Habitant" is French Canadian for "country dweller," (more or less). This soup, made with dried whole yellow peas, was basic sustenance for the farmers of Quebec for centuries.

Soak the whole peas overnight in water to cover generously (no need to soak split peas, if using); drain. Mix the soaked peas in a large heavy pot with the broth, onion, carrots, celery, garlic, bay leaf, parsley, and allspice. Simmer about 2 hours, or until the peas are tender. If you are using the liquid smoke and/or soy bacon chips, add them during the last 30 minutes or so. Taste for salt and pepper.

Purée about 3 cups of the soup in the pot with a hand immersion blender or transfer to a food processor or blender and purée, leaving an opening in the lid for steam to escape to prevent an explosion. Cover the opening loosely with a folded cloth as you purée. Add the puréed soup back to the soup pot along with the sesame oil. Mix well. Serve hot.

2 cups dried whole yellow peas
OR 1 cup whole plus 1 cup split yellow peas for a thicker soup

8 cups vegetable broth

1 large onion, chopped

2 carrots, diced

½ cup chopped celery

2 cloves garlic, crushed

1 bay leaf

2 tablespoons chopped parsley

½ teaspoon ground allspice

Salt and freshly ground pepper to taste

1 teaspoon liquid smoke and/or about 1 tablespoon soy "bacon" chips or bits, or 2 tablespoons chopped vegetarian "Canadian back bacon" or "ham" (optional)

1 tablespoon toasted sesame oil

PER SERVING:			
Calories	185	FIBER	11.7g
Total Fat	11g	Carbohydrate	31g
Saturated Fat	0g	Protein	11g
Calories from fat	23%	Sodium	18mg

MEATLESS TSAR'S ARMY BORSCHT

Makes 8 servings

This is a meatless borscht that originally was made with beef. The original recipe is from an old cookbook (I can't even remember the name now) by a Russian woman, who claimed that her recipe was the one used in the tsar's army. Who knows? Anyway, I replaced the beef with soy sauce (for "meaty" flavor) and protein and fiber-rich split red lentils. The lentils melt into the soup but give it fiber and body. Grate a raw beet into the soup during the last five minutes before serving, to revive the bright color. This is a wonderful soup!

Heat the oils in a large heavy soup pot. Stir-fry the onions, garlic, and celery leaves over medium-high heat until the onion starts to soften. Add all of the remaining ingredients except salt and the grated raw beet. Simmer, covered, about 4 hours. Taste for seasoning. Five minutes before serving, add the grated raw beet. Serve with a dollop of nondairy sour cream.

1½ tablespoons extra-virgin olive oil

½ tablespoon toasted sesame oil

2 large onions, sliced

2 cloves garlic, chopped

1 handful chopped celery leaves

8 cups water

1 (14-ounce) can diced tomatoes, with juice

½ small head green cabbage, shredded

2 peeled, diced beets

½ cup soy sauce

½ cup split red lentils

Freshly ground black pepper to taste

Salt to taste

1 small raw beet, peeled and grated

Nondairy sour cream, for garnish

PER SERVING:			
Calories	114	FIBER	4.7g
Total Fat	4g	Carbohydrate	16g
Saturated Fat	1g	Protein	6g
Calories from fat	31%	Sodium	1115mg

Navy Bean Soup

Makes 6 servings

This is a vegetarian version of the classic Senate Bean Soup, served in the U.S. Senate dining room. It's a wonderful winter soup, and it doesn't get much cheaper than this!

Soak the beans overnight in water to cover. Add 1 teaspoon of the salt, cloves, peppercorns, and bay leaf. Bring to a boil, reduce the heat and simmer, covered, 2 hours.

Run through a food mill or blend in the pot with an immersion blender or transfer to a food processor or blender; blend coarsely, leaving an opening in the lid for steam to escape to prevent an explosion. Cover the opening loosely with a folded cloth as you purée.

In a heavy skillet, heat the oils over medium-high heat. Add the celery, onion, and carrot. Stir-fry until the onion is tender; add to the soup. If the soup is too thick, add broth until desired consistency is reached. Simmer 20 minutes. Add the soy sauce and tomato paste, and taste for salt and pepper. Stir in liquid smoke and/or "bacon," if using, and oregano.

VARIATION: For a thicker soup, use 2 cups dried white beans.

1 cup dried navy or small white beans

6 cups water

1 teaspoon salt

1-3 whole cloves

6 peppercorns

1 bay leaf

1 tablespoon extra-virgin olive oil

1 tablespoon toasted sesame oil

⅓ cup chopped celery with leaves

1 small onion, minced

⅓ cup shredded carrot

Vegetable broth as needed to thin soup (optional)

1½ tablespoons soy sauce

1½ tablespoons tomato paste or ¼ cup tomato sauce

Salt and freshly ground black pepper to taste

1 teaspoon liquid smoke and/or about 1 tablespoon soy "bacon" chips or bits, or 2 tablespoons chopped vegetarian "Canadian back bacon" or "ham" (optional)

¼ teaspoon dried oregano (optional)

PER SERVING:			
Calories	165	FIBER	4.9g
Total Fat	5g	Carbohydrate	23g
Saturated Fat	1g	Protein	8g
Calories from fat	27%	Sodium	627mg

CALDO GALLEGO
(Spanish Kale and Potato Soup)

Makes 6-8 servings

Kale and potatoes are made for each other, as you'll see when you try this wonderful soup. In Spain (and also Portugal, where it's called "Caldo Verde"), this soup contains a spicy (but very fatty) sausage called chorizo, which is seasoned with garlic, dry red wine, chile, paprika, and cumin. I add these seasonings to the soup instead of using chorizo. Cubes of turnip are another characteristic Spanish touch. NOTE: Don't be alarmed over the large amount of garlic in this soup—it mellows out considerably during cooking.

In a heavy soup pot, heat the oils over medium-high heat. Add the onion and garlic and stir-fry several minutes, or until the onion softens. Add a little water as needed to keep from sticking. Add the bay leaf, paprika, cumin, and pepper flakes and stir 2 minutes. Add all of the remaining ingredients, bring to a boil, cover and simmer about 15 minutes, or until vegetables are tender. Taste for salt and pepper.

VARIATION: For the Portuguese version, Caldo Verde, use 4 potatoes, omit the turnip, and reduce the kale to ½ pound.

1 tablespoon extra-virgin olive oil

½ tablespoon toasted sesame oil

1 large onion, chopped

1 head garlic, peeled and minced (about 10 jarred cloves or 2-4 tablespoons jarred minced garlic)

1 bay leaf

1 teaspoon paprika

1 teaspoon ground cumin

¼-½ teaspoon dried red pepper flakes or pinch of cayenne pepper

6 cups vegetable broth

10-12 ounces kale, turnip greens, or collard greens, trimmed and chopped

2 medium red-skinned potatoes, unpeeled, thinly sliced

1 medium turnip, peeled and cut in ½-inch dice

1½ cups or 1 (19-ounce) can cooked white kidney (cannellini) beans, drained

¼ cup dry red wine or 1 tablespoon balsamic vinegar

2-3 sliced spicy vegetarian weiners (optional)

Salt and freshly ground pepper to taste

PER SERVING:			
Calories	166	FIBER	5.4g
Total Fat	4g	Carbohydrate	27g
Saturated Fat	0g	Protein	6g
Calories from fat	21%	Sodium	41mg

FARRO MINESTRONE
with Squash and Greens

Makes 8 servings

Farro is an ancient Italian grain that is related to wheat. It has been making a comeback in recent years. There is some controversy over whether or not it is actually a type of spelt, but, since I can't find farro where I live, I have used spelt instead, with success.

Simmer the spelt kernels in water to cover for 40-90 minutes or until tender; set aside.

In a heavy soup pot, heat the oils over medium-high heat. Add the onion, carrots, celery, and garlic and stir-fry until the onion starts to soften. Add a little water as needed to keep from sticking. Add the cooked spelt plus any remaining cooking liquid and all of the remaining ingredients except salt, pepper, olive oil, and Parmesan. Simmer, covered, about 30 minutes, or until the vegetables are tender. Taste for salt and pepper and serve with the olive oil and/or Parmesan to sprinkle on top.

½ cup whole spelt or farro kernels

1 tablespoon extra-virgin olive oil

1 tablespoon toasted sesame oil

1 large onion, chopped

2 medium carrots, chopped

½ cup chopped celery with leaves

4 cloves garlic, minced

3 cups or 2 (15-ounce) cans cooked pinto or white kidney (cannellini) beans

5 cups vegetable broth

1 (14-ounce) can diced tomatoes with juice

2 cups cubed, peeled winter squash

2 medium red-skinned potatoes, unpeeled, diced

4 cups trimmed and sliced greens—kale, Swiss chard, collards or turnip greens

1 teaspoon dried marjoram or crumbled sage

1 teaspoon dried thyme or rosemary

1 bay leaf

Salt and freshly ground pepper to taste

Extra-virgin olive oil and/or soy Parmesan cheese to sprinkle on top

1 tablespoon soy "bacon" chips or bits, or 2 tablespoons chopped vegetarian "Canadian back bacon" or "ham" (optional)

PER SERVING:			
Calories	236	FIBER	11g
Total Fat	4g	Carbohydrate	44g
Saturated Fat	1g	Protein	10g
Calories from fat	15%	Sodium	114mg

GUMBO Z'HERBES

Makes 8 servings

This evidently was originally a vegetarian Lenten dish, but meat and seafood are usually added nowadays. Here's a low-fat version that is absolutely scrumptious!

Brown flour in a dry cast-iron skillet over medium heat, stirring constantly, until it is the color of coffee grounds; do not burn.

In a large pot, heat the oil. Sauté the onions, celery, bell pepper, and garlic SLOWLY over medium-low heat until the onion softens. Stir in the browned flour. Stir in the broth. Add the greens, spices, liquid smoke (if using), "bacon" chips, and black-eyed peas or sausages. Bring to a boil, reduce heat, and simmer, covered, 1 hour.

Mix the rice with 3 cups water and ½ teaspoon salt in a covered saucepan and bring to a boil. Reduce heat to low and cook, covered tightly, 45 minutes.

Taste the gumbo for salt and pepper. Serve each bowl with about ¾ cup cooked rice.

⅔ cup unbleached flour

2 tablespoons olive oil

2 large onions, minced

1 cup minced celery

1 medium bell pepper (any color), seeded and chopped

2 cloves garlic, chopped, or more to taste

6 cups vegetable broth

12 cups chopped greens (Traditionally, 5-12 different kinds of greens are used)*

1 bay leaf

½ teaspoon filé powder (optional)

¼ teaspoon each cayenne pepper, dried thyme, dried marjoram

Pinch each ground cloves and allspice

1 teaspoon liquid smoke (optional)

1 tablespoon soy "bacon" chips or bits, OR 2 tablespoons chopped vegetarian "Canadian back bacon" or "ham"

2-3 cups cooked and drained black-eyed peas or chickpeas OR browned spicy vegetarian "sausages" or weiners

Salt and freshly ground pepper to taste

2 cups raw long-grain brown rice, such as brown basmati

½ teaspoon salt

*You can use mustard, turnip or collard greens, spinach, parsley, beet tops, rapini, escarole, kale, chard, cabbage, Chinese broccoli, broccoli, etc.

PER SERVING:			
Calories	260	FIBER	7.8g
Total Fat	5g	Carbohydrate	46g
Saturated Fat	1g	Protein	11g
Calories from fat	17%	Sodium	196mg

Chinese Velvet Corn Soup

Makes 4 servings

Corn is not the first thing that comes to mind when you think of Chinese cooking, but, when it was imported from the Americas, the Northern Chinese took to it readily. This soup is extremely popular, even at formal banquets, but it's quick and simple to make.

In a medium bowl, toss the tofu with 1 tablespoon of the soy sauce, brown sugar, and ½ teaspoon cornstarch. Heat a large heavy wok or skillet over high heat. Add oil. Reduce heat to medium-high, add tofu and soy sauce mixture, and stir-fry several minutes until liquid is absorbed; do not brown tofu. Set aside.

Mix the broth, corn, peas, the remaining 1 tablespoon soy sauce, and the soy "bacon," if using, in a medium saucepan. Bring to a boil, reduce heat to a simmer, and cook until the peas are just tender. Stir in the tofu, pepper, and cornstarch mixture. Simmer until thickened, drizzle with oil, and serve.

NOTE: Creamed corn contains no dairy products.

6-7 ounces firm tofu, diced or julienned

2 tablespoons soy sauce

½ teaspoon brown sugar

½ teaspoon cornstarch

½ tablespoon oil

4 cups vegetable broth

1 (14 to .15-ounce) can creamed corn

1 cup frozen baby peas

1 tablespoon soy "bacon" chips or bits, or 2 tablespoons chopped vegetarian "Canadian back bacon" or "ham" (optional)

White pepper to taste

1 tablespoon cornstarch dissolved in 1 tablespoon cold water

1 teaspoon toasted sesame oil

PER SERVING:			
Calories	182	FIBER	5.5g
Total Fat	6g	Carbohydrate	27g
Saturated Fat	1g	Protein	9g
Calories from fat	29%	Sodium	751mg

OKRA GUMBO

Makes 8 servings

I consulted many gumbo recipes and finally came up with a hearty, lower-fat vegetarian version that I really like. Like Gumbo Z'Herbes (page 102), I use browned flour instead of fatty roux, and serve it with fiber-rich brown basmati rice.

½ cup unbleached flour

1 tablespoon toasted sesame oil

8 ounces frozen baby okra, trimmed and sliced in ½-inch thick rounds

2 tablespoons extra-virgin olive oil

1 large onion, chopped

2 large cloves garlic, minced

1 stalk celery, sliced

1 small bell pepper (any color), seeded and chopped

5 green onions, chopped

4 cups vegetable broth

1 (14-ounce) can diced tomatoes with juice

1 large bay leaf

1 teaspoon dried thyme

¼ teaspoon cayenne pepper

1 tablespoon soy "bacon" chips or bits, OR 2 tablespoons chopped vegetarian "Canadian back bacon" or "ham"

1 teaspoon liquid smoke (optional)

2-3 cups cooked and drained black-eyed peas or chickpeas OR browned spicy vegetarian "sausages"; or plain or spicy vegetarian weiners

Salt and freshly ground black pepper to taste

2 cups dry long-grain brown rice

½ teaspoon salt

Brown flour in a dry cast-iron skillet over medium heat, stirring constantly, until it is the color of coffee grounds; do not burn.

Heat the oil in a large heavy pot. Sauté the okra over medium heat 5 minutes; set aside.

In the same pot, heat the olive oil. Add the onion, garlic, celery, bell pepper, and green onions. Sauté until the onion softens. Stir in the browned flour, broth, tomatoes, okra, bay leaf, thyme, cayenne, black pepper, "bacon" chips, liquid smoke (if using), and black-eyed peas. Bring to a boil, reduce heat to a simmer, and cook 1 hour.

Mix the rice with 3 cups water and ½ teaspoon salt in a covered saucepan and bring to a boil. Reduce heat to low and cook, covered tightly, 45 minutes.

Taste the gumbo for salt and pepper. Serve each bowl with about ¾ cup cooked rice.

GUMBO VARIATION

FILÉ GUMBO: Use ¼ cup flour. Omit the okra. Use 1 large bell pepper and 2 stalks celery. Five minutes before serving, add 1-1½ tablespoons filé powder. Let stand 5 minutes, then serve as above.

PER SERVING: (Okra Gumbo)			
Calories	238	FIBER	7g
Total Fat	6g	Carbohydrate	39g
Saturated Fat	1g	Protein	8g
Calories from fat	22%	Sodium	228mg

EASY SAVORY WHITE BEAN AND CORN SOUP

Makes 6 servings

This soup was inspired by a recipe in Sunset *magazine. It's great with focaccia or a wedge of leftover pizza.*

In a medium pot, steam-fry the onion and garlic about 5 minutes or until the onion softens. Add the beans and broth and mash the beans coarsely with a potato masher. Add all of the remaining ingredients and simmer 10 minutes. Taste for seasoning and serve.

1 large onion, minced

2 cloves garlic, minced

2 (15-ounce) cans or 3 cups cooked white kidney (cannellini) beans, Great Northern, or navy beans, drained

2 cups vegetable broth

1 (14-ounce) can diced tomatoes with juice

8 ounces canned creamed corn (about 1 cup)

1 teaspoon dried savory

½-1 teaspoon salt

Freshly ground pepper to taste

PER SERVING:			
Calories	159	FIBER	8g
Total Fat	1g	Carbohydrate	32g
Saturated Fat	0g	Protein	9g
Calories from fat	5%	Sodium	396mg

MAINLY BEANS

Beans, dried peas, and lentils contain on average 21 to 25 percent protein; soybeans contain even more, between 35 and 48 percent. They are high in iron, calcium, potassium, zinc, magnesium, and B vitamins. They are also low in fat. But what beans are known for is their fiber content. All legumes are not only rich in the insoluble fiber, the type that aids the digestive system, but also in the soluble fiber that helps lower cholesterol and triglycerides in the bloodstream.

BASIC BEAN COOKING

Many cooks are intimidated by the idea of cooking beans, confused by the process—to soak or not to soak?—and so many prefer to just purchase canned beans. But cooking beans is not difficult, and cooking your own can help you save money, keep you from hauling heavy cans home from the market, and provide you and your family with a less-processed, lower-sodium food that's high in fiber and nutrition. If the idea of beans intimidates you, read on to dispel the mysteries and start cooking.

Beans can be cooked without soaking, but it will take longer; plus soaking, discarding the soaking water, and cooking the beans in fresh water does reduce the chance of intestinal problems that beans are famous for (see page 107 for more about this).

First, sort through the beans to remove any pebbles or other foreign material; rinse them, and then soak the beans in three times their volume of water.

The *overnight soak* is the most popular method (and, in my opinion, the best, especially for soybeans). Use 3-4 cups water per cup of dry beans, and set the beans aside in a cool place overnight.

The *quick-soak* method involves cooking the beans a bit before soaking them. Place the beans and water (use 3 cups of water per cup of dry beans) in a large saucepan. Bring to a boil and boil 2 minutes. Remove from the heat, cover, and let stand 1 hour.

The *pressure-soak* method cooks the beans under high pressure in a pressure cooker 1 minute, using 4 cups water per cup dry beans. Quick-release the pressure under cold running water.

Whichever soaking method you use, for ease of digestion discard the soaking water (nutrient loss is minimal), and add fresh water for cooking. Cook beans in plain water until the skins are soft, then add salt and desired seasonings. Beans are done when they are tender enough to be easily mashed onto the roof of your mouth with your tongue. (Undercooked beans can cause intestinal distress, particularly to young children and the elderly.) For a delicious pot of beans that can be used in other recipes or eaten alone for their own goodness, add salt to taste and, if you wish, a bay leaf or two, a few whole peeled garlic cloves, a chopped onion, and maybe a sprig of thyme. The flavored broths from chickpeas and soybeans are particularly delicious and can be used as broth in other recipes.

There are several ways to cook beans: The pressure cooker is indispensable for spur-of-the-moment bean cooking—beans can be cooked without soaking in a fraction of the time of stovetop cooking. Follow the directions for your cooker. By the way, you do not have to add oil to beans when pressure-cooking in the new cookers.

Beans can be cooked in a slow-cooker, but it can be tricky. This is my method: Cook the soaked and drained beans in a pot on the stovetop 40 to 60 minutes or until the beans are almost tender; drain. Transfer the beans to the slow-cooker with the other recipe ingredients. (Chop any vegetables you are using quite small to ensure even cooking.) Use only ¾ of the liquid called for. (Slow-cookers do not evaporate liquid as oven-baking does.) Cook on HIGH 5-6 hours or on LOW 10-12 hours. Do not lift the lid during cooking.

Microwave ovens do not significantly save time when cooking dried beans. Save microwaving for recipes that start with cooked or canned beans, or for thawing or reheating beans.

THE MUSICAL FRUIT

The oligosaccharides, raffinose, and stachyose in the carbohydrate portion of beans are what cause gas in the intestine, because humans lack an enzyme called alpha-galactosidase that is necessary to hydrolyze them. Instead, they enter the lower intestines intact, where they are metabolized by bacteria, producing gases such as carbon dioxide, hydrogen, and methane. There is considerable variability in how different beans affect different people. Individuals may have no problems with certain beans and yet are very uncomfortable with others. (Anasazi beans, adzuki beans, mung beans, and lentils are reportedly easiest for most people to digest.) This may be because of different levels of bacterial flora in the lower intestine. The more you eat beans, the better your body seems to handle them, so increase your intake slowly if you are not used to eating beans. Fermented bean products such as soy sauce, tempeh, and miso are practically devoid of gas-producing abilities.

If you have a lot of gas when eating beans, there are traditional methods of alleviating it. Some people swear by cooking the sea vegetable kombu with their beans (about a 4-inch strip per pot of beans), or using digestive spices such as ginger, cumin, and fennel when cooking beans. The Mexican herb epazote is also reported to ease digestion. I take a cup of fennel tea after a bean meal! Soaking beans and discarding the soaking water, along with sufficient cooking in fresh water, will help reduce gas. And by the way, beans are not the only foods that can trigger what is often called "bean bloat." Cabbage family vegetables, carrots, grapes, and other high-fiber foods can trigger a similar reaction.

Border Beans and Refried Beans

Makes 6-8 servings

This is my vegetarian version of a recipe from my late mother-in-law, Ruth Clark. I use it as a basic bean recipe for any Mexican type of dish, but I love them plain, too.

3 cups pinto beans

8 cups vegetable broth

5 cloves garlic, chopped

1-3 dried red chiles (she used chile pequins), crumbled

2 teaspoons dried oregano

A few dashes of liquid smoke

2 tablespoons soy "bacon" chips or bits (optional)

2 tablespoons toasted sesame oil

Salt to taste

Soak the pinto beans in 9 cups water overnight; drain. Discard the soaking water and place the soaked beans in a large pot with all of the remaining ingredients except the oil and salt. Bring to a boil, boil about 3 minutes, reduce heat, and simmer, covered, 2-3 hours or until the beans are very tender. Add the oil and taste for salt. These beans are a bit soupy, but the broth is delicious!

TO PRESSURE COOK: Cook at 15 pounds pressure for 30 minutes. To cook un-soaked beans, use 11 cups water and 8 bouillon cubes in at least a 6-quart cooker. Pressure cook at 15 pounds pressure for 1 hour.

TO MAKE REFRIED BEANS (no fat necessary), drain cooked beans, reserving some of the cooking liquid. Add as many beans as you need and a small amount of the broth to a very large, heavy skillet over high heat. Mash beans with a potato masher while cooking the broth down. When beans are mashed, stir constantly with a wooden spoon to keep beans from sticking to the pan. Cook until beans are desired consistency. Easy!

PER SERVING:

Calories	267	FIBER	14.6g
Total Fat	5g	Carbohydrate	44g
Saturated Fat	1g	Protein	14g
Calories from fat	16%	Sodium	3mg

MOLÉ PINTO BEANS

Makes 6 servings

Molé is a distinctive savory Mexican sauce with chocolate as the surprise ingredient. You can buy molé mixes and pastes at the market, but they are usually high in fat. This one is not. And a blender makes it so easy to prepare! Eat it with salad and rice, soft fresh polenta, or tortillas. Use as a filling for enchiladas; the sauce by itself, simmered for 15-30 minutes, makes an excellent enchilada sauce and is also delicious on fried tofu and tempeh or your favorite vegetarian "cutlet."

In a blender, mix all of the ingredients except 1½ cups of the broth and the beans. Blend until very smooth. Add the remaining ½ cup broth and blend again. Pour the sauce over the beans in a non-stick pot or skillet and simmer, covered, 15-20 minutes.

3 large tomatoes, cut into chunks or
1 (28-ounce) can tomatoes, drained or
¼ cup tomato paste plus ⅔ cup water

2 cups vegetable broth

1 green bell pepper, seeded and diced

3 tablespoons unsweetened cocoa

3 tablespoons toasted sesame seeds OR
1½ tablespoons tahini or nut butter

2 tablespoons masa harina or cornmeal

2 tablespoons raisins

1½ tablespoons dark chili powder
(preferably ancho chili powder)

3 cloves garlic, peeled

1 teaspoon each salt and sugar
or alternative

½ teaspoon ground anise

¼ teaspoon ground coriander

⅛ teaspoon cinnamon

Dash each of black pepper and
ground cloves or allspice

3 (15-ounce) cans or 4½ cups
cooked pinto beans, drained

PER SERVING:			
Calories	245	FIBER	13.9g
Total Fat	4g	Carbohydrate	44g
Saturated Fat	1g	Protein	13g
Calories from fat	14%	Sodium	368mg

TUSCAN BEANS
with Tomato and Sage

Makes 6 servings

Tuscans are sometimes called "mangiafagioli" or "bean-eaters" by their fellow Italians because they love beans so much! And why not, when they taste this good?

In a medium pot or skillet, heat the olive oil. Sauté the garlic and sage until almost browned. Add the beans, broth, and tomatoes, and simmer 15-25 minutes. Taste for salt and pepper. Serve with crusty bread.

¼ cup extra-virgin olive oil

3 cloves garlic, chopped

5 fresh sage leaves

4 cups cooked or 2¼ (15-ounce) cans cannellini, great Northern, cranberry, borlotti, or pinto beans, drained

1 cup vegetable broth

1 pound ripe plum tomatoes, chopped, or 1 (14-ounce) can diced tomatoes

Salt and freshly ground pepper to taste

¼ teaspoon dried red pepper flakes (optional)

Bean Tips

➤ One 15 or 16-ounce can of beans contains about 1½ cups cooked beans. For this reason, I freeze my home-cooked beans in 1½-cup, 3-cup, and 4½-cup containers.

➤ To thaw beans, place the container of frozen beans in a pan of hot water, then dump the contents into a colander (save the liquid if you like) and finish thawing by running hot tap water over the beans until they separate.

➤ The "star" of quick-cook legumes is the split red lentil (or the Indian masoor dal). These tiny orange lentils have had their seed coats removed, so they cook without soaking in as little as 10 minutes. Substitute them for white beans, chickpeas, etc., in pâtés, pureés, soups, etc.

➤ One cup dehydrated bean flakes (available in bulk in many natural food stores) soaked for 5 minutes with ¾ cup boiling water yields 1 cup mashed beans.

➤ Frozen soaked beans cook more quickly—in about ¾ of the time—than soaked beans that have not been frozen.

➤ Soybeans soften properly only if frozen first or pressure-cooked after soaking.

PER SERVING:

Calories	234	FIBER	9.2g
Total Fat	10g	Carbohydrate	28g
Saturated Fat	1g	Protein	10g
Calories from fat	38%	Sodium	9mg

Vegetarian "Meat Loaf"

Makes 6-8 servings

This simple recipe was adapted from one from my friend Dee Selchelski of Atlanta, Georgia. With the exception of beans, most vegetarian foods with high concentrations of protein are not very high in fiber, so I have adapted this recipe to add more fiber. It's simply delicious and open to lots of experimentation with seasonings. This is good cold or hot, and makes great sandwiches!

Preheat the oven to 375°F.

In a medium bowl, dissolve the bouillon in the boiling water. Stir in the ketchup and soy sauce. Add the soy protein and let stand 5-10 minutes or until the liquid is absorbed. Add all of the remaining ingredients except the topping. Mix well. Pack into an oiled 10-inch shallow glass casserole or a 9 x 5-inch loaf pan. Spread the Topping sauce evenly over the top. Bake 45 minutes.

Vegetarian bouillon for 4 cups broth

2 cups boiling water

½ cup ketchup

2 tablespoons soy sauce

2 cups textured soy protein granules

½ cup oat bran

½ cup wheat or rice bran

¼ cup ground flaxseeds

2 tablespoons extra-virgin olive oil or toasted sesame oil

1 tablespoon nutritional yeast flakes

1 teaspoon each garlic granules, onion powder, and dried thyme (or other herb of choice)

Freshly ground pepper to taste

Ketchup, tomato sauce, or barbecue sauce as topping

PER SERVING:			
Calories	176	FIBER	5.9g
Total Fat	6g	Carbohydrate	20g
Saturated Fat	1g	Protein	15g
Calories from fat	30%	Sodium	497mg

BLACK BEAN AND CORN BURGERS
with Chipotle Crème

Makes 8 servings

NOTE: A food processor does the best job of mincing and chopping vegetables for this recipe.

Mix all of the Chipotle Crème ingredients together in a small bowl; cover and refrigerate.

To make the burgers, heat a large non-stick skillet over high heat. Spray with oil from a pump sprayer, or oil the pan lightly with olive oil or toasted sesame oil. Add the onions and stir-fry until softened, adding a little water, wine, or broth as necessary to keep from sticking. Add the garlic and mushrooms and stir-fry until the mushroom liquid evaporates. Mix mushroom mixture in a large bowl with all of the remaining burger ingredients. Chill the mixture if you are not making the burgers right away.

Form 12-16 ½-inch thick patties; coat lightly in bread crumbs. Heat a nonstick skillet over medium heat. Brush or spray it with olive oil or toasted sesame oil. Cook the patties about 5 minutes per side or until browned on both sides. Serve hot with the Chipotle Crème.

CHIPOTLE CRÈME

1 cup nondairy sour cream

1 tablespoon fresh lemon juice or 2 tablespoons fresh lime juice

½ teaspoon adobado sauce (from canned chipotle chiles), or to taste

¼ teaspoon salt

BURGERS

2 medium onions, finely minced

2 cloves garlic, minced or crushed

2 cups finely minced fresh mushrooms

2 cups frozen corn kernels, thawed, squeezed dry, and chopped

¼ cup minced cilantro

2 canned chipotle chiles in adobado sauce, mashed

2 teaspoons ground cumin

1 teaspoon vinegar

2 teaspoons salt

4 cups cooked or canned black beans, rinsed and well-drained and mashed

½ cup stone-ground cornmeal

1 cup finely ground fresh whole grain bread crumbs

More bread crumbs for coating burgers

PER SERVING:			
Calories	264	FIBER	10.3g
Total Fat	7g	Carbohydrate	42g
Saturated Fat	5g	Protein	11g
Calories from fat	23%	Sodium	661mg

Indian Black-Eyed Peas

with Dill and Eggplant

Makes 6 servings

This is my take on a vegetarian dish from Gujarat Province of India (renowned for its wonderful vegetarian cuisine) and a good example of the way Indian cuisine makes use of fresh herbs as well as spices.

Heat an oiled heavy skillet, pot, or wok. Add the onion, garlic, cumin, mustard, and red pepper flakes. Cook, stirring constantly, over medium-high heat, adding a little water as necessary to keep it from sticking, about 10 minutes or until the onion softens. Add the tomatoes, bay leaves, eggplant, black-eyed peas, dill, paprika, and curry powder. Mix well and bring to a boil. Reduce the heat and cook, uncovered, 15 minutes. Taste for salt and serve with brown basmati rice.

1 large onion, minced

1 teaspoon minced garlic

¾ teaspoon ground cumin

½ teaspoon dry mustard

½ teaspoon dried red pepper flakes

1½ cups chopped fresh or canned tomatoes

4 bay leaves

1 medium eggplant, unpeeled, cut into 1-inch cubes

2 (15-ounce) cans or 3 cups cooked black-eyed peas, drained

2-3 bunches fresh dill, with stems, chopped (or 2-3 tablespoons dried dill weed)

1 teaspoon paprika

2 teaspoons curry powder or garam masala

1½ cups water or vegetable broth

Salt to taste

Cooked brown basmati rice

PER SERVING:			
Calories	135	FIBER	7.9g
Total Fat	1g	Carbohydrate	26g
Saturated Fat	0g	Protein	8g
Calories from fat	6%	Sodium	10mg

Red Lentil Dal

Makes 6 servings

Red lentils, or masoor dal, require no soaking, and they cook in 10-15 minutes! Serve the dal over rice and steamed vegetables or with curried vegetables and rice, for a deliciously inexpensive and simple Indian-style meal. Thin any leftover dal with water, tomato juice, and salt to taste. For "noodle" soup, sliver raw pappadams (round Indian lentil wafers) with scissors and add to the soup to cook for a few minutes.

This dish is seasoned with a tempered oil and spice mixture known as a "chaunk." I use a flavorful expeller-pressed oil in Indian dishes instead of ghee (clarified butter).

1½ cups split red lentils (masoor dal), rinsed and drained

4 cups water

1½ teaspoons salt

CHAUNK

¼ cup extra-virgin olive oil or peanut oil or a mixture

1 teaspoon cumin seeds

1 teaspoon ground turmeric

½ teaspoon yellow mustard seeds

6 whole cloves

Small cinnamon stick

¼ teaspoon powdered ginger

¼ teaspoon ground coriander

Pinch of cayenne

Mix the lentils, water, and salt in a medium saucepan. Bring to a boil; reduce heat and simmer, covered, 20 minutes or until very soft. Skim off any foam.

Meanwhile, to make the chaunk, heat the oil in a nonstick heavy skillet or dry cast-iron skillet. Add the spices and fry, stirring constantly, for a few minutes, being careful not to burn them. Add to the lentils and mix well.

TO MAKE A FAT-FREE CHAUNK, dry-fry the spices in a dry hot pan, stirring constantly. When you can smell them, add ¼ cup broth and stir around for a minute, then remove from the heat.

When the lentils are cooked soft, pour in the chaunk and stir. (If you like it thicker, simmer it longer, uncovered.)

NOTE: Served cold, this makes an excellent cracker or pita spread or pâté.

PER SERVING:			
Calories	194	FIBER	7.8g
Total Fat	9g	Carbohydrate	20g
Saturated Fat	1g	Protein	9g
Calories from fat	41%	Sodium	365mg

VEGETARIAN FEIJOADA
(Brazilian Black Beans)

Makes 8-10 servings

Serve with Spicy Greens (page 130) and sliced peeled oranges, Louisiana hot sauce, vinegar or lemon juice, and sliced onions marinated in vinegar for several hours.

Place the dried beans in a large pot with all of the remaining feijoada ingredients except salt and oil. Boil 5 minutes; reduce heat and simmer, covered, 2-3 hours or until beans are tender. Taste for salt; drain, reserving broth.

To pressure-cook in a large pressure cooker (or in a smaller cooker in 2 batches), cook all of the feijoada ingredients except salt and oil at 15 pounds pressure for 40 minutes.

About an hour before serving, heat a large heavy saucepan with a tight lid. Add the rice and stir over high heat with a wooden spoon 2 minutes. Add the water and salt. Bring to a boil, cover and reduce heat to low. Simmer 45 minutes. Remove from heat and let stand about 15 minutes before serving.

Mound the beans in the center of a large serving platter and surround them with the rice. If you like, drizzle them with the sesame oil. Pass bean broth in a pitcher.

FEIJOADA

4 cups dried black beans

12 cups vegetable broth

4 onions, chopped

1 (28-ounce) can diced tomatoes, with juice

4 large cloves garlic, minced

2 teaspoons dried oregano

1 teaspoon liquid smoke

½ teaspoons cayenne pepper

Salt to taste

¼ cup toasted sesame oil (optional)

RICE

4 cups long-grain brown rice or brown basmati rice

6 cups water

1 teaspoon salt

NOTE: For a wonderful soup, mix leftover beans, rice, and Spicy Greens with broth. I like to add chunks of cooked sweet potato to this as well. Cook 30 minutes.

PER SERVING:			
Calories	392	FIBER	17.8g
Total Fat	2g	Carbohydrate	76g
Saturated Fat	1g	Protein	19g
Calories from fat	4%	Sodium	391mg

30-Minute Vegetarian Chili

Makes 6 servings

Despite the speed of preparation and the addition of vegetarian "hamburger" and vegetables, this is very authentic-tasting chili. This freezes well.

In a large pot, sauté the garlic in the olive oil over medium heat just until it begins to turn color. Add the chili powder, oregano, cumin, and red pepper flakes and cook 2 minutes more. Add all of the remaining ingredients except the salt and cornmeal.

Simmer about 20 minutes. During the last 5 minutes, sprinkle with the cornmeal and stir it in. Taste for salt.

Serve with rice, bread, polenta, tortillas, or cornbread.

PER SERVING:			
Calories	275	FIBER	14.1g
Total Fat	4g	Carbohydrate	50g
Saturated Fat	1g	Protein	15g
Calories from fat	13%	Sodium	1070mg

6 cloves garlic, chopped or crushed

1 tablespoon extra-virgin olive oil

3 tablespoons chili powder
(preferably dark, such as ancho)

1 tablespoon dried oregano

½ tablespoon ground cumin

½ teaspoon dried red pepper flakes

1 (28-ounce) can diced
tomatoes, with juice

4½ cups cooked or 3 (15-ounce) cans
pinto beans, drained

1½ cups hot water or bean broth from
home-cooked beans
(don't use canned bean liquid)

2 cups vegetarian "hamburger crumbles"

1 green bell pepper, seeded and chopped

1 cup corn kernels

1 cup or more diced unpeeled zucchini
or other summer squash

¼ cup soy sauce

1 tablespoon each red pepper sauce,
onion powder, and
unsweetened cocoa powder

1 teaspoon sugar

2 tablespoons cornmeal or masa harina

½ teaspoon salt or to taste

Beans with Sage and Lemon, Tuscan-Style

Makes 4-6 servings

This is one of the simplest and most delicious bean dishes that I know of. Originally, the beans were baked in an empty Chianti bottle in a brick oven on baking day. (A casserole in a modern oven may not be as rustic, but the beans taste just as good!) They were often eaten cold, but they are delicious hot, as well. The beans are eaten with lemon juice and olive oil drizzled on top. Use leftovers as a delicious spread.

Soak the beans overnight or for about 8 hours in plenty of cold water. When ready to cook, drain and rinse the beans.

Preheat the oven to 325°F. Place the beans in a 2-quart casserole and pour in enough hot water to cover them by about ¼ inch. Add the sage leaves, garlic, and olive oil. Partially cover and bake 1½ hours or until the beans are very tender. Season to taste with salt and pepper and serve warm or at room temperature with lemon wedges and olive oil.

2 cups dried cannellini or Great Northern beans

3 sage leaves

2 cloves garlic, coarsely chopped

1 tablespoon extra-virgin olive oil plus more for garnish

Salt and freshly ground pepper to taste

1 lemon, cut into wedges

PER SERVING:			
Calories	253	FIBER	12.3g
Total Fat	4g	Carbohydrate	38g
Saturated Fat	1g	Protein	15g
Calories from fat	15%	Sodium	4mg

ROSEMARY BEANS: Substitute 3 tablespoons chopped fresh rosemary for the sage. Omit the lemon and substitute toasted sesame oil for the olive oil garnish. Serve hot.

GIANT LIMA BEANS
Peasant Style

Serves 4-6

Giant lima beans (sometimes called "gigantes") are delicious even to those of us who claim not to like ordinary limas. They really blend well with tomatoes, herbs, and a little hot pepper. This Italian recipe, and the Greek versions on page 119, are such favorites in our family that I often take them to potlucks.

Soak the beans overnight or for about 8 hours in plenty of cold water. When ready to cook, drain and rinse the beans.

Preheat the oven to 350°F.

In a large heavy nonstick skillet, heat the oil over medium-high heat. Sauté the onions, carrot, and celery (if using) until onions are translucent. Mix the beans and the sautéed vegetables in a large pot, medium Dutch oven, or small oval roasting pan with a lid. Pour 2 cups water into the skillet and scrape up any browned bits, then pour the water into the pot with the bean mixture. Add the peppers, garlic, dried basil, salt, black pepper, and red pepper flakes, if using. Cover and bake 2 hours or until the beans are soft. Add more water if they get too dry. Taste for salt and pepper.

1 pound dried giant lima beans ("gigantes")

2-3 tablespoons extra-virgin olive oil

3 onions, coarsely chopped or sliced

1 carrot and 1 celery stalk, chopped (optional)

2 cups water

3 large bell peppers, seeded and cut into strips

2 pounds fresh plum tomatoes, chopped, or 1 (28-ounce) can diced tomatoes, with juice

4 garlic cloves, minced or crushed

2 teaspoons dried basil (or 2 tablespoons minced fresh basil)

1½ teaspoons salt

Freshly ground black pepper to taste

¼-½ teaspoon dried red pepper flakes (optional)

TOPPING

1 cup fresh whole grain bread crumbs

½ cup Soy Parmesan or minced hazelnuts (filberts) or walnuts

¼ cup ground flaxseeds

2 tablespoons minced fresh Italian parsley

During the last 15 minutes or so of cooking, mix the fresh basil, bread crumbs, soy Parmesan, flaxseeds, and parsley and sprinkle over the top.

Serve hot with crusty bread and steamed or sautéed greens.

PLAKI (a typical Greek dish): Omit the bell peppers. Add the carrot and celery. You can also add a diced potato. Use 1 teaspoon dried basil, and a handful of chopped parsley. Omit topping.

MACEDONIAN VERSION: Add 1 teaspoon oregano and 1 teaspoon ground cumin instead of the basil. Omit topping. Use the chile option.

PER SERVING:			
Calories	334	FIBER	13g
Total Fat	11g	Carbohydrate	47g
Saturated Fat	1g	Protein	16g
Calories from fat	29%	Sodium	888mg

POLPETTINE DI FAGIOLI
(Italian-Style Bean Patties)

These make a good antipasto dish as well as a main course (you can serve them with a light tomato sauce); cold patties are good in sandwiches.

This is more of a guide than a recipe. You can use leftover cooked beans, canned beans, or beans that you have cooked especially for this.

Drain and mash cooked or canned cannellini, borlotti, Roman, cranberry, or pinto beans. Add salt and freshly ground pepper, along with soy Parmesan to taste. Stiffen the mixture with stale or toasted whole grain bread crumbs. The mixture is easier to handle if you chill it for a few hours. Form the mixture into small patties, coat with dry, fine whole grain bread crumbs, and fry in extra-virgin olive oil until golden brown on both sides. Drain on paper.

MAPLE BAKED BEANS

Makes 6 servings

Two Native American ingredients, maple syrup and anasazi beans (which reputedly do not cause the same gastric distress that many dried beans do), make this a delectable main dish, sure to be a family favorite all year long. Smoky toasted sesame oil takes the place of the traditional fatback.

2 cups dried anasazi beans
(If you can't find these, you can use navy, pea or pinto beans)

6 cups water

2-4 tablespoons toasted sesame oil

1 small onion, peeled

1 cup pure maple syrup (the darker Grade B is the best for this recipe)

2 teaspoons salt

1 teaspoon dry mustard

Soak beans overnight or for at least 8 hours in plenty of cold water. When ready to cook, drain and rinse the beans. Cook the beans in a large pot with 6 cups water. Bring to a boil, reduce heat, and simmer 10 minutes. Drain the beans, reserving the cooking water.

Preheat the oven to 300°F.

Place the beans in a casserole or pot. Stir in the oil. Insert the onion in the center of the beans. In a medium bowl, mix 1 cup of the maple syrup with ¾ cup of the reserved bean liquid, the salt, and the dry mustard; pour over the beans. Add just enough reserved bean liquid so beans are covered. Cover the pot and bake 2 hours. Add the remaining reserved bean liquid, stir well and bake 1½ hours. Uncover and bake 30 minutes more or until the beans are very soft and the liquid is absorbed. Taste to see if it is sweet enough. If not, add a bit more maple syrup. Serve hot.

SLOW-COOKER METHOD: Cook the soaked beans in water to cover on the stovetop 40-60 minutes or until the beans are tender; drain, reserving bean liquid. Chop onion. Add beans and ¾ cup reserved bean liquid to slow cooker with all of the remaining ingredients. Cook on HIGH 5-6 hours or on LOW 10-12 hours.

PER SERVING:

Calories	401	FIBER	7.6g
Total Fat	8g	Carbohydrate	73g
Saturated Fat	1g	Protein	12g
Calories from fat	17%	Sodium	717mg

YEMISER WAT
(Ethiopian Spicy Lentils)

Makes 8 servings

Serve this delicious lentil stew with steamed long-grain brown rice.

1 cup dried brown lentils

2 tablespoons extra-virgin olive oil or peanut oil

1 cup minced onions

2 cloves garlic, minced

1 tablespoon paprika

1 teaspoon ground cumin

1 teaspoon red wine vinegar

½-1 teaspoon dried red pepper flakes

Pinch each of ground cardamom, ginger, cinnamon, cloves, allspice, coriander, and nutmeg

Pinch of fenugreek (optional)

1 (28-ounce) can diced tomatoes, drained

1 cup vegetable broth

¼ cup tomato paste

1 cup frozen green peas

Salt to taste

Rinse the lentils, cover them generously with water in a medium pot, and bring to a boil. Reduce the heat, cover, and simmer about 45 minutes, adding more water if necessary. Don't let them get mushy.

Meanwhile, heat the oil in a large heavy skillet. Add the onions and garlic and sauté over medium heat until soft. Add the spices and sauté several minutes. Add the tomatoes, broth, and tomato paste and simmer 15 minutes. Add the peas and taste for salt. Simmer 10 minutes more.

PER SERVING:

Calories	151	FIBER	7.6g
Total Fat	4g	Carbohydrate	22g
Saturated Fat	1g	Protein	8g
Calories from fat	23%	Sodium	186mg

PASTA WITH CHICKPEAS

Makes 6 servings

This very simple Italian peasant dish is one of my very favorite winter comfort foods. I am constantly amazed by how such common foods can yield such wonderful flavor.

8 cups vegetable broth, plus more as needed

2½-3 cups cooked or canned chickpeas, drained

2-3 carrots, diced

8 ounces whole grain shell pasta or macaroni

3 cloves garlic, minced

1 tablespoon extra-virgin olive oil, plus more for garnish

1-2 handfuls chopped greens (optional)

Dried red pepper flakes

Bring the broth to a boil in a large pot. Add the chickpeas, carrots, and pasta; reduce heat to a simmer. Simmer until carrots and pasta are tender, about 15 minutes.

In a small skillet, sauté the garlic over medium heat in 1 tablespoon olive oil just until it begins to turn beige; don't let it get golden or brown. Add this to the soup along with greens, if using. Add more broth as needed to reach desired consistency. Serve with olive oil and red pepper flakes for garnish.

PER SERVING:			
Calories	295	FIBER	10.2g
Total Fat	5g	Carbohydrate	53g
Saturated Fat	1g	Protein	13g
Calories from fat	15%	Sodium	19mg

Black Bean and Potato Tacos

Makes 18 small tacos

This sounds like an odd combination, but it's actually an authentic Mexican one—and very tasty.

Cut up the potatoes into small chunks. Brown them in a large nonstick skillet with a little bit of olive oil, adding salt and taco seasoning to taste. Keep warm in a low oven.

Heat the Bean Dip in a glass casserole in the microwave or the oven. Heat the taco shells according to the package directions. Have the salsa, chopped greens, and nondairy sour cream ready. To assemble each taco (you can do this, or place everything on the table and let the diners do their own), smear some bean dip in the bottom of the taco shell. Add a scoop of potatoes, some greens, a dollop of salsa, and sour cream to top it off. Get out the napkins and enjoy!

10 medium potatoes, cooked until tender

Extra-virgin olive oil

Salt to taste

Taco seasoning to taste

1 recipe Spicy Mexican Bean Dip made with black beans (p. 62)

18 taco shells

CONDIMENTS

2½ cups shredded lettuce or green cabbage

About 2 cups of your favorite salsa

Nondairy sour cream for garnish

PER SERVING: (including condiments)

Calories	216	FIBER	5.6g
Total Fat	5g	Carbohydrate	36g
Saturated Fat	1g	Protein	6g
Calories from fat	20%	Sodium	329mg

Quick Chili "Beef" Pie

Makes 6 servings

This is a meatless version of a dish I used to make as a teenager. Kids like this—it's not highly spiced. Creamed corn (which actually contains no cream) adds moisture, flavor, and fiber to the corn dumplings. TIP: Freeze the rest of the can of creamed corn in ½ cup portions if you have no immediate use for it.

For the filling, in a large heavy skillet, heat the oil over medium-high heat. Sauté the onion and bell pepper until the onion begins to soften. Add the "hamburger crumbles" and break them up, mixing with the onions. Add all of the remaining filling ingredients; cover, reduce heat to a simmer, and cook 10 minutes.

For the corn dumplings, mix the biscuit mix with the cornmeal in a small bowl. Make a well in the center and add the creamed corn and milk. Mix with a fork, and quickly incorporate the dry mixture. Do not beat. Spoon the dough onto the hot bean mixture. Cover and cook 12 minutes more. Serve immediately.

FILLING

1 tablespoon extra-virgin olive oil

1 medium onion, minced

½ medium green bell pepper, seeded and chopped

2 cups vegetarian "hamburger crumbles"

1 tablespoon chili powder

1 teaspoon salt

½ teaspoon garlic granules

1 tablespoon soy sauce

1 cup tomato sauce

3 cups cooked or 2 (15-ounce) cans red kidney or pinto beans, drained

1 cup water

CORN DUMPLINGS

¾ cup biscuit mix or ¾ cup unbleached flour, ½ teaspoon salt, and 2 teaspoons baking powder

½ cup stone-ground cornmeal

½ cup cream-style corn

½ cup nondairy milk

PER SERVING:			
Calories	313	FIBER	11.9g
Total Fat	4g	Carbohydrate	53g
Saturated Fat	1g	Protein	18g
Calories from fat	11%	Sodium	1081mg

MAINLY VEGETABLES

When we think of fiber, grains come immediately to mind, but vegetables are a major source of fiber as well—or they should be. Nutritionists urge us to eat—at the very least—5 servings of vegetables a day (1 serving is about ½ cup cooked), but the preferred amount is actually 9 to 11 servings! Sound like too much? Not if you put vegetables into the starring role for many of your weekly meals. This chapter has not only easy and delicious side dishes starring vegetables, but delectable main-course vegetable recipes that will keep your family coming back for more!

KIMA
(Vegetarian "Pakistani Hash")

Makes 6 servings

This is an easy family meal—all you need with it is rice. Children love it, oddly enough—at least, my children did. Maybe it's the potatoes, carrots, and peas along with the "burger"—all familiar foods. Unpeeled carrots and potatoes, along with high-fiber peas, make this a flavor-and-fiber-rich, low-fat meal. With steamed brown basmati rice, chutney, and a salad, it's even better! This makes a lot, but the leftovers are great!

2 onions, chopped

2 cloves garlic, minced

2 cups packed vegetarian "hamburger crumbles"

2 stalks celery, diced

4 medium thin-skinned potatoes, diced small

4 medium carrots, diced small

2 cups frozen baby peas

2 tablespoons curry powder

3 tablespoons soy sauce or mushroom soy sauce

1 teaspoon salt

Pepper to taste

4-6 fresh or 8-12 canned tomatoes, chopped OR ⅓ cup tomato paste mixed with ½ cup water

Hot cooked brown basmati rice

Preheat the oven to 350°F. Put a pot of brown basmati rice on to cook.

Use a large (12 to 14-inch) skillet or casserole that can be used both in the oven and on top of the stove, if you have one. Otherwise, you will have to transfer the mixture from a large skillet to a large oven-proof casserole before baking.

Lightly oil the bottom of the skillet with your fingertips. Over high heat, stir-fry the onions and garlic, adding a splash of water if necessary to keep from sticking. When the onions start to get soft, add the remaining ingredients, stirring well. Turn the heat up and bring the mixture to a boil, then remove from the heat. Cover the skillet (use foil or a round pizza pan if you have no lid for your skillet), or scrape the mixture into an oven-proof casserole, cover, and bake for 30 minutes. The mixture should be fairly dry.

PER SERVING:			
Calories	206	FIBER	7.5g
Total Fat	1g	Carbohydrate	38g
Saturated Fat	0g	Protein	13g
Calories from fat	4%	Sodium	889mg

MATTAR TOFU

Makes 4 servings

One of the best-loved Indian restaurant dishes is Mattar Panir, a tomatoey mixture of green peas and cubes of fresh cheese. Firm tofu is an easy and convincing substitute for the fatty cheese, and peas are an excellent source of fiber. Serve this with brown basmati rice for a complete meal.

Spray the tofu cubes with a little olive oil or peanut oil from a spray pump. In a large nonstick skillet over high heat, fry the tofu until the cubes are golden on 2 sides. Remove from pan and set aside.

Add the ginger and garlic to the hot skillet and stir-fry over high heat with a little bit of water for 1 minute. Add the onion and stir-fry until it is soft, about 5 minutes, adding a splash of water as needed to keep from sticking. Add the seasonings and water and stir well. Add the tomatoes, peas, tofu, and sugar, and simmer 10-15 minutes. Serve with rice.

12 ounces firm tofu, cut into ½-inch cubes

2 tablespoons grated fresh ginger

1 tablespoon chopped garlic

1 medium onion, minced

1 teaspoon salt

1 teaspoon turmeric

1 tablespoon garam masala or curry powder

1 teaspoon ground coriander

Pinch of cayenne pepper

¼ cup water or broth

1 (14-ounce) can diced tomatoes, with juice

1½ cups frozen baby peas

1 teaspoon sugar

Hot cooked brown basmati rice

PER SERVING:			
Calories	208	FIBER	6.5g
Total Fat	8g	Carbohydrate	21g
Saturated Fat	1g	Protein	18g
Calories from fat	34%	Sodium	711mg

Artichoke Stew
with Mushrooms and Carrots

Makes 8-10 servings

This Greek-style vegetable stew, redolent of white wine, lemon, and dill, can be made ahead and reheated.

Heat the oil in a large heavy pot: Sauté the onion, garlic, carrots, and mushrooms until the onions soften and the vegetables are beginning to brown. Add the artichokes, broth, wine, and dill weed. Bring to a boil, cover, reduce heat and simmer 30 minutes. Add the parsley, lemon juice, and salt and pepper. Stir in the starch mixture until it has thickened (cornstarch has to boil, potato starch does not). If it is still not thickened sufficiently, stir in another tablespoon of starch dissolved in cold water and heat again. Serve hot.

VARIATION

For an everyday dish, omit the mushrooms and substitute 2 pounds small thin-skinned, unpeeled potatoes, cut into "nuggets" or chunks. Because of the natural potato starch, you may not need as much thickening for this version. Eat as a one-dish meal with crusty bread.

¼ cup extra-virgin olive oil

2 cups chopped onion

6 cloves garlic, chopped

8 large carrots, cut into 1-inch chunks

1 pound whole small mushrooms

2 (9-ounce) packages frozen artichoke hearts or 2 (14-ounce) cans artichoke hearts in water

3 cups vegetable broth

1 cup dry white wine

1 tablespoon dill weed

½ cup chopped fresh parsley

Juice of 1 lemon

Salt and freshly ground pepper to taste

1 tablespoon potato starch or cornstarch dissolved in ¼ cup water, plus more if needed to reach desired consistency

PER SERVING:

Calories	186	FIBER	4.4g
Total Fat	6g	Carbohydrate	21g
Saturated Fat	1g	Protein	5g
Calories from fat	29%	Sodium	288mg

Garlic Green Beans

Makes 4 servings

Heat a large wok or heavy skillet over medium heat. Add the oil, garlic, and ginger, if using; stir-fry 2 minutes or just until the garlic begins to change color; do not brown. Add the green beans and toss well. Increase heat to high and cook about 2 minutes. Add the soy sauce and sugar and stir-fry 2 minutes. Add the sherry. Reduce heat to medium and cook, uncovered, about 10 minutes, stirring occasionally, until the beans are tender (add a little bit of vegetable broth if the beans appear too dry). Serve hot, room temperature, or cold as a salad. Top with toasted sesame seeds, if you like.

2 tablespoons oil

3 cloves garlic, crushed or minced

1 tablespoon minced fresh ginger (optional)

1 pound fresh (trimmed) or frozen (thawed) whole (not cut) green beans

4 teaspoons light soy sauce

1 teaspoon sugar

1 tablespoon dry sherry

Vegetable broth as needed

PER SERVING:			
Calories	109	FIBER	3.9g
Total Fat	7g	Carbohydrate	10g
Saturated Fat	1g	Protein	3g
Calories from fat	57%	Sodium	234mg

Chinese Chili Green Beans

Makes 4 servings

If you are using fresh beans, blanch about 2 minutes in boiling water, drain and place them in cold water.

Heat a large wok or heavy skillet over high heat. Add the oil and reduce heat to medium. Add the garlic and red pepper flakes and stir-fry 1 minute. Drain the green beans, and add them to the pan, along with the soy sauce and sugar. Increase heat to high. Stir-fry 3-5 minutes, until the beans are tender. Sprinkle with the sesame oil and serve.

1 pound small fresh green beans, trimmed or frozen small whole (not cut) green beans, thawed

1 tablespoon oil

2 cloves garlic, crushed

½ teaspoon dried red pepper flakes

2 tablespoons light soy sauce

½ teaspoon sugar

1 teaspoon toasted sesame oil

PER SERVING:			
Calories	86	FIBER	3.9g
Total Fat	5g	Carbohydrate	9g
Saturated Fat	1g	Protein	3g
Calories from fat	52%	Sodium	355mg

SPICY SOUTHERN-STYLE GREENS

Makes 8-10 servings

You can use your favorite greens or a mixture of collards, turnip greens (my favorite), kale, mustard greens, or spinach.

4-5 pounds fresh greens*

2 large onions, minced

6 cloves garlic, chopped

6 cups vegetable broth

Few dashes of liquid smoke

2 large red bell peppers, seeded and diced

Salt and freshly ground black pepper to taste

Red pepper sauce, vinegar, and toasted sesame oil

Soy bacon chips or chopped vegetarian "back bacon" or "ham" (optional)

In a large, lightly oiled heavy-bottomed pot, steam-fry the onions and garlic over high heat until limp, adding a splash of water as needed just to keep from sticking. Add the broth and bring to a boil. Add the greens in batches, except spinach, if using (see note below). Fill the pot, then cook at high heat until the greens go limp enough to push down into the broth. Add another batch and repeat until all the greens are used. Sprinkle with liquid smoke.

Cover and simmer 45-60 minutes or until the greens are tender, adding spinach and bell peppers after 25 to 40 minutes. Taste for salt and pepper. Serve the hot greens and "pot liquor" in bowls with red pepper sauce, vinegar, and sesame oil. Sprinkle with soy bacon, if using.

NOTE: Spinach cooks much more quickly than the other greens, so add it about 20 minutes before other greens are tender.

*How to Clean Greens

Fill your kitchen sink with lukewarm water and add the greens, trimmed of roots, tough stems, and yellowed leaves. (If using spinach, wash it separately.) Swish the greens around to remove grit. Take the greens out, leaving the grit in the water. Drain the greens well in a colander. Repeat this procedure as many times as necessary, depending upon the size of your sink. (This looks like A LOT of greens, but they cook down quite a bit.)

PER SERVING:			
Calories	138	FIBER	5.7g
Total Fat	2g	Carbohydrate	28g
Saturated Fat	0g	Protein	8g
Calories from fat	13%	Sodium	100mg

Nutritious Greens

Collard greens are the preferred green leafy vegetable in the American South and in West Africa, but in some Northern areas, they are hard to find unless you grow them yourself. One cup of cooked collards contains 357 mg. of calcium, among other things, so, like the other greens mentioned here, this easy-to-grow vegetable is worth planting in your garden.

The traditional way to cook Southern greens is with smoked pork. Here I use vegetable broth, liquid smoke, and lots of onions and garlic, for lots of flavor without the fat. (Soy bacon chips or chopped vegetarian "back bacon" or "ham" can be sprinkled on top, if you like.) Red bell pepper mixes with the greens to add color, and a little toasted sesame oil drizzled over the finished product adds a smoky flavor, too.

The large amount of broth used results in a nutritious "pot liquor" which is served with the greens in bowls. Even though the greens are cooked for quite a long time, compared to the way we usually cook greens, nothing is lost when the "pot liquor" is enjoyed along with the greens.

FLORENTINE BABY PEAS

Makes 8 servings

All peas are an excellent source of fiber. If you cannot find very tiny, freshly picked early peas, use frozen baby peas, not mature peas.

In a large heavy skillet, cook the peas with about ⅓ cup water over medium heat, covered, 5 minutes for frozen peas, about 10 minutes for fresh peas, or just until tender and still bright green; drain. Stir in the parsley, "back bacon" or "ham," and the margarine. Toss well with salt to taste and a few twists of the pepper mill. Serve immediately.

2 (10-ounce) packages frozen baby peas, thawed, or 4 pounds (unshelled weight) early peas, shelled

¼ cup minced fresh parsley

¼ cup minced vegetarian "Canadian back bacon" or vegetarian "ham"

2 tablespoons nondairy margarine

Salt and freshly ground black pepper

PER SERVING:

Calories	91	FIBER	3.7g
Total Fat	4g	Carbohydrate	11g
Saturated Fat	1g	Protein	4g
Calories from fat	39%	Sodium	65mg

Vegetable Goulash

Makes 8 servings

This is a very elegant Hungarian-style stew, made with dry red wine as the liquid (use a good brand of nonalcoholic wine, such as Ariel, if you like). It's so easy to put together—and then it just cooks itself in the oven! Serve the Goulash over whole wheat or brown rice fettucine, tossed with a bit of olive oil or nondairy margarine, with nondairy sour cream on the side.

2 tablespoons extra-virgin olive oil

1 large green bell pepper, seeded and cut into 1-inch squares

1 large onion, thickly sliced

4 cloves garlic, minced

1 medium eggplant, unpeeled, cubed

12 medium mushrooms, halved

1 (28-ounce) can tomatoes, with juice

2 bay leaves

8 medium red-skinned potatoes, unpeeled, quartered

3 large carrots, cut into chunks

2 cups dry red wine (can be nonalcoholic)

1 tablespoon dill weed

1 tablespoon paprika

1 tablespoon dark or mushroom soy sauce

1 teaspoon sugar

1½ teaspoons salt, plus more to taste

Freshly ground black pepper to taste

¼ cup minced fresh parsley (optional)

Preheat the oven to 350°F.

In a large, heavy ovenproof pot, heat the olive oil. Sauté the bell pepper, onion, and garlic until the onion starts to soften. Add the eggplant, mushrooms, tomatoes (squishing them up a bit first), bay leaves, potatoes, carrots, wine, dill weed, paprika, soy sauce, sugar, and salt. Bring to a boil, cover and bake 1½ hours. Stir well and taste for salt and pepper. You may need as much as ½ tablespoon more salt. Add the parsley, if using.

PER SERVING:			
Calories	289	FIBER	6.4g
Total Fat	4g	Carbohydrate	44g
Saturated Fat	1g	Protein	6g
Calories from fat	12%	Sodium	711mg

7 Vegetable Couscous

Makes 6-8 servings

This has a long list of ingredients, but it is actually a very simple stew served with couscous.

In a large heavy pot, heat the oil over high heat. Add the onion, garlic, and chile pepper and sauté 5 minutes. Add the broth, tomato sauce, and seasonings and bring to a boil. Add the vegetables, raisins, and chickpeas. Cover and simmer 15 minutes. Taste for salt.

While the stew is cooking, toast the couscous in a hot nonstick or lightly oiled skillet or medium saucepan over medium heat, stirring 2 minutes. (This will keep the grains separate and dry.) Remove from the heat and stir in the boiling broth. Cover and let stand 10 minutes.

Fluff the couscous with a fork and mound it on a warm serving platter. With a slotted spoon, lift out the vegetables and chickpeas and arrange around the couscous. Ladle some of the cooking broth over the vegetables and couscous.

Sprinkle with the parsley. Serve with the hot sauce and the remaining broth.

PER SERVING:			
Calories	322	FIBER	7.8g
Total Fat	5g	Carbohydrate	60g
Saturated Fat	1g	Protein	10g
Calories from fat	13%	Sodium	217mg

2 tablespoons extra-virgin olive oil

1 onion, diced

2 cloves garlic, minced

1 small dried red chile pepper, crumbled

4 cups vegetable broth

¼ cup tomato sauce or
1 tablespoon tomato paste

1 teaspoon cinnamon

½ teaspoon paprika

¼ teaspoon Spanish saffron

¼ teaspoon ground ginger

½ pound thin-skinned red potatoes, unpeeled, cut into 1½-inch cubes

½ pound carrots, cut into
½-inch thick slices

1 medium sweet potato, peeled

1 medium zucchini or summer squash, unpeeled, cut into 1½-inch chunks

1 red or green bell pepper, seeded and cut into 1½-inch squares

1 (14-ounce) can quartered artichoke hearts in water, drained

½ cup raisins

1 (15-ounce) can or 1½ cups cooked chickpeas, drained

Salt to taste

2⅔ cups whole wheat couscous

4 cups boiling vegetable broth

¼ cup chopped fresh parsley, for garnish

Red pepper sauce, for garnish

CIAMBOTTA
(Southern Italian Vegetable Stew)

Makes 4 servings

You might see this spelled "giambotta" or "cianfotta," but whichever way, it's delicious— deceptively so, because the ingredients are so simple. You can vary the vegetables and amounts according to what's in your garden or market. Serve with a good crusty whole grain bread to sop up the good juices. Leftovers are delicious!

Toss the eggplant in a colander with the 2 teaspoons salt; set aside in the sink until it starts to sweat out the bitter juices. Rinse, drain, and pat dry, squeezing a little.

In a large pot, heat the oil. Add the onion, garlic, and celery. Stir-fry over high heat about 5 minutes, adding a little water as necessary to keep from sticking. Add the basil and stir-fry for a minute; add the tomatoes. When mixture comes to a simmer, add the eggplant, potatoes, and ½ teaspoon salt. Stir, bring to a boil, reduce heat, and simmer, covered, 15 minutes. Add the zucchini and peppers and simmer 15 minutes more or until the vegetables are tender.

Taste for salt and pepper, transfer to a warm serving bowl, and let stand 15 minutes before serving.

½ pound eggplant,* unpeeled and cut into 1-inch cubes

2 teaspoons salt

1 tablespoon extra-virgin olive oil

1 large onion, thinly sliced

5 large cloves garlic, minced

1 stalk celery, thinly sliced

1 large handful fresh basil leaves, chopped

1 (14-ounce) can crushed tomatoes

¾ pound thin-skinned potatoes, unpeeled, cut into 1x2-inch pieces

½ teaspoon salt

½ pound zucchini,** unpeeled, cut into ½-inch rounds

1 large or 2 small sweet red or yellow bell peppers, seeded and cut into ½-inch strips

Salt and freshly ground black pepper

*Instead of eggplant, you can use mushrooms.

**Instead of zucchini you can use any summer squash, or try using cauliflower or fennel root.

PER SERVING:

Calories	174	FIBER	6.0g
Total Fat	4g	Carbohydrate	33g
Saturated Fat	1g	Protein	5g
Calories from fat	20%	Sodium	446mg

STUFFED SQUASH
with Wild Rice and Chanterelles

Makes 6 servings

Chanterelle mushrooms are widely available. If you can't find them, use fresh shiitakes, oyster mushrooms, creminis, or even ordinary button mushrooms.

Preheat the oven to 350°F. If using small squash, cut them in half and scoop out and discard the seeds. Place cut-side down in a shallow baking pan with ½ inch hot water. Bake 40 minutes or just until tender. If using large squash, preheat the oven to 400°F. Slice the top off the squash and scoop out and discard the seeds, scraping the interior well. Place squash in a baking pan, put the top back on, and bake 1 hour or just until tender. It's difficult to be exact with large squash because the cooking time varies with the type and thickness of the squash.

To make the stuffing, bring the broth to a boil in a medium pot. Wash the wild rice in a colander under running water. When the broth boils, add the washed wild rice, bring to a boil, cover, reduce heat and simmer 55 minutes or until tender.

Stir-fry the chanterelles, green onions, celery, and onion in the oil in a large non-stick or lightly oiled skillet over high heat until tender and slightly browned. Add

3 small winter squash (about 1¼ pound each) or 1 medium-large winter squash (about 6-8 pounds)

STUFFING

3½ cups light vegetable broth

1½ cups wild rice

4 cups sliced cleaned chanterelle mushrooms

1 cup chopped green onions

4 stalks celery, sliced

1 cup minced onion

2 tablespoons extra-virgin olive oil

½ teaspoon dried thyme

½ teaspoon dried marjoram

Salt and freshly ground black pepper to taste

the cooked wild rice, herbs, and salt and pepper to taste.

Mound the stuffing into the cooked squash and place in a shallow baking pan. (If there is any stuffing left over, place it around the squash.) Cover. Bake the small squash 20 minutes; the large squash, 45-60 minutes. Serve hot with your favorite gravy.

PER SERVING:			
Calories	214	FIBER	7.3g
Total Fat	6g	Carbohydrate	38g
Saturated Fat	1g	Protein	5g
Calories from fat	25%	Sodium	180mg

PUTTENAIO

Makes 6 servings

This is a bit like an Italian ratatouille with potatoes added. It can be served hot or cold, and leftovers make a delicious antipasto dish or first course. All you need is a good crusty bread to mop up the juices, and perhaps a glass of red wine!

1 tablespoon olive oil

1 large eggplant, cut into 1-inch chunks

1 large thin-skinned potato, unpeeled and cut into 1-inch chunks

1 small carrot, unpeeled and sliced

1 stalk celery, diced

2 medium zucchini, unpeeled, sliced

1 large green bell pepper, seeded and cut into 1-inch squares

1 medium onion, thinly sliced

2 cloves garlic, crushed

¼ cup vegetable broth

1 (28-ounce) can diced tomatoes with juice

1 teaspoon salt

1 small handful each Italian parsley and either rosemary, thyme, or basil, chopped

Freshly ground black pepper to taste

Heat the oil in a large heavy pot. Add the eggplant, potato, carrot, celery, zucchini, green pepper, onion, and garlic, and cook 5 minutes, stirring in the broth as needed to keep it from sticking. Add the tomatoes and salt. Bring to a boil, then turn down, cover and simmer 45 minutes. If there is still a lot of juice, uncover and cook over high heat (watching carefully!) until juices are reduced to a syrup. Add the fresh herbs, reduce heat, cover and simmer 15 minutes. Taste for salt and pepper.

PER SERVING:

Calories	125	FIBER	5.1g
Total Fat	3g	Carbohydrate	24g
Saturated Fat	0g	Protein	4g
Calories from fat	21%	Sodium	587mg

Stir-Fried Tofu and Snow Peas

Makes 3-4 servings

A Cantonese favorite.

Mix the tofu, stir-fry sauce, soy sauce, sherry, cornstarch, and white pepper together and set aside. Heat a large wok, stir-fry pan, sauté pan, or heavy skillet over high heat. When it's hot, add the oil. When the oil is hot, add the tofu and garlic and stir-fry until the tofu begins to brown. Add the mushrooms, bamboo shoots, and the snow peas. Stir-fry about 2 minutes, adding drops of water if the mixture begins to stick.

In a small bowl, mix together all of the Cooking Sauce ingredients except the cashews. Add the Cooking Sauce to the tofu mixture and stir until it bubbles and thickens. Stir in the nuts and serve immediately.

PER SERVING:			
Calories	292	FIBER	3.9g
Total Fat	18g	Carbohydrate	20g
Saturated Fat	3g	Protein	15g
Calories from fat	55%	Sodium	700mg

TOFU

6-7 ounces firm or extra-firm tofu, cut into ½-inch cubes

1 tablespoon vegetarian stir-fry sauce*

2 teaspoons light soy sauce

2 teaspoons dry sherry

2 teaspoons cornstarch

Dash white pepper

1 tablespoon oil

1 clove garlic, minced

VEGETABLES

4 medium dried shiitake or Chinese black mushrooms, soaked, stemmed, and thinly sliced (save soaking water)

½ cup sliced canned bamboo shoots or sliced celery

½ pound fresh or frozen snow peas, trimmed and stringed

COOKING SAUCE

½ cup water

1 tablespoon dry sherry

1 tablespoon light soy sauce

1 tablespoon vegetarian stir-fry sauce*

1 tablespoon cornstarch

1 teaspoon toasted sesame oil

¼ teaspoon sugar

½ cup toasted cashews or blanched almonds

* A mushroom-based, vegetarian version of Chinese oyster sauce.

Pasta Alla Primavera

Makes 6 servings

My version of this famous spring vegetable pasta dish (which is actually more vegetables than pasta) is gorgeously creamy, but is much lower in fat than most recipes. Broiling the vegetables first adds a delicious flavor. Substitute any other vegetables that seem appropriate, or that proliferate in your garden or produce store.

Make the Bechamel Sauce. Cook the pasta according to package directions until al dente; drain.

Preheat the broiler. Place all of the vegetables except the peas and green onions in a large, shallow roasting pan and toss with the olive oil. Place the pan 3-4 inches from the broiler and roast the vegetables until they are slightly charred. Turn, add the peas and green onions, and broil until crisp-tender and slightly charred around the edges.

Add the basil and Bechamel Sauce to the vegetables and stir gently. Taste for salt and pepper. Add the cooked pasta, toss well, and serve hot with the Parmesan.

I recipe medium Bechamel Sauce (p. 84)

I pound uncooked egg-free fettucine "nests," or linguine, spaghetti, or other favorite pasta

I medium onion, sliced

2 large cloves garlic, chopped

I pound thin asparagus, trimmed and sliced diagonally

½ pound button or cremini mushrooms, sliced

2 small zucchini or other summer squash, cut into ¼-inch rounds

I small carrot, peeled, halved lengthwise and sliced diagonally into ⅛-inch slices, or 4 sliced baby carrots

6 ounces cauliflower, cut into thin slices

I cup baby peas or 2 cups sugar snap peas, cut into I-inch slices

5 green onions, chopped

1-2 tablespoons extra-virgin olive oil

2 tablespoons chopped fresh basil

Salt and pepper to taste

Nondairy Parmesan cheese

PER SERVING:			
Calories	284	FIBER	8.3g
Total Fat	8g	Carbohydrate	45g
Saturated Fat	1g	Protein	14g
Calories from fat	25%	Sodium	120mg

FLORENTINE STUFFED BAKED POTATOES

Makes 6 servings

This is a great way to serve baked potatoes as a main dish, and the fiber-rich skins are very appetizing this way!

6 medium baking potatoes, baked

1 tablespoon olive oil
or nondairy margarine

1 large onion, chopped

2 cups sliced mushrooms

1 cup Bechamel Sauce (p. 84)
or nondairy sour cream

1 pound spinach or other fresh greens,
cooked, squeezed dry, and chopped,
or 1 (10-ounce) package frozen chopped
spinach, thawed and squeezed dry

Chopped garlic and other fresh herbs to
taste (optional)

¼ cup nondairy Parmesan cheese

Salt, freshly ground black pepper, and
chopped parsley to taste

Preheat the oven to 400°F.

Cut the potatoes in half lengthwise. Scoop out the cooked potato into a bowl. Place the potato skin halves right-side up on a baking sheet.

Heat the oil or margarine in a nonstick skillet over medium heat. Add the onion and sauté until it starts to soften. Increase the heat and add the mushrooms. Sauté until they brown a bit. Set aside.

Mash the potato in the bowl well with a potato masher. Beat in the Bechamel Sauce. Add the chopped spinach, sautéed onion and mushrooms, and chopped garlic and herbs, if using. Add the Parmesan and mix well. Taste for salt and pepper and add parsley as desired. Pile the mixture generously back into the potato skins. Spray the tops with oil from a pump sprayer. Bake for about 10 minutes, or until heated through. Serve immediately.

PER SERVING:			
Calories	206	FIBER	5.9g
Total Fat	4g	Carbohydrate	35g
Saturated Fat	1g	Protein	9g
Calories from fat	17%	Sodium	157mg

COLCANNON
(Irish Mashed Potatoes with Kale)

Makes 6 servings

3 pounds russet or other good mashing potatoes

2 pounds kale
OR green or Savoy cabbage

2 cups minced leeks or green onions

¾ cup nondairy milk

Salt and pepper to taste

Cut the potatoes into chunks and boil in water or broth to cover until tender, but not mushy.

Meanwhile, wash and trim the kale or cabbage, discarding any tough stems. Chop and steam 5-10 minutes or until tender.

Cool and gently squeeze out the water. In a lightly oiled skillet, stir-fry the leeks until softened, adding a splash of water or broth as needed to keep them from sticking.

Drain the potatoes well and mash with a potato masher. Beat in the nondairy milk, then the cooked kale or cabbage and leeks. Taste for salt and pepper. Serve hot.

"CHAMP" OR "STELK" (IRELAND) OR "CHAMPITT TATTIES" (SCOTLAND): Instead of the cabbage or kale, mix the potatoes with about 2 cups cooked, mashed baby peas and use the green onions instead of leeks.

"RUMBLEDETHUMPS" (SCOTLAND): Use green or Savoy cabbage instead of kale.

"TATTIES 'N' NEEPS" (SCOTLAND) OR "PUNCH-NEP" (ENGLAND): Instead of the cabbage or kale, use mashed peeled boiled, steamed, or roasted turnips. Use chives instead of leeks or green onions.

"CLAPSHOT" (SCOTLAND): Instead of the cabbage or kale, use mashed peeled boiled, steamed, or roasted rutabagas.

PER SERVING:			
Calories	304	FIBER	8.1g
Total Fat	2g	Carbohydrate	66g
Saturated Fat	0g	Protein	11g
Calories from fat	5%	Sodium	85mg

INDIAN POTATO AND PEA CURRY

Makes 6 servings

This is one of my family's favorite dishes. It's so easy and inexpensive to make, and the ingredients are common ones we always have around. With rice or chapatis and dal, it makes a simple meal. It's traditionally made with quite a bit of ghee (clarified butter), but you won't miss that at all!

1 teaspoon cumin seeds

1 teaspoon turmeric

1 teaspoon ground coriander

½ teaspoon yellow mustard seeds

¼ teaspoon cayenne pepper

6 medium thin-skinned potatoes, unpeeled, cut into ½-inch dice

2 cups vegetable broth

⅔ cup frozen peas, thawed

1 cup nondairy sour cream

Salt to taste

Heat a large heavy skillet, lightly oiled, over high heat and add all of the spices. Stir constantly for 1-2 minutes. Add the potatoes and toss well. Add 1-2 table-spoons water to keep the mixture from sticking and burning. Stir-fry briefly until potatoes start to brown. Add the broth, bring to a boil, reduce the heat, and sim-mer, covered, 30 minutes, stirring occa-sionally.

When the potatoes are tender, add the peas and simmer 5 minutes more. Stir in sour cream. Taste for salt. Serve immedi-ately.

VARIATION: Omit the potatoes and use a large head of cauliflower, broken into very small florets. When you add the cau-liflower to the pan, add 1 clove garlic, crushed, to the spices. Substitute 1 cup broth and 1 cup canned diced tomatoes or 1 large fresh tomato, diced, for the 2 cups broth. Cook just until the cauliflower is tender. Omit sour cream, and add 2 table-spoons lemon juice along with the peas. Taste for salt.

PER SERVING:			
Calories	144	FIBER	3.8g
Total Fat	1g	Carbohydrate	30g
Saturated Fat	0g	Protein	4g
Calories from fat	6%	Sodium	11mg

Pâté Chinois
(Quebec-Style Vegetarian Shepherd's Pie)

Makes 4 servings

This is the shepherd's pie (with the odd, but traditional name) that my husband Brian grew up with. The traditional addition of corn to the mashed potatoes adds fiber as well as variety to the dish.

Preheat oven to 400°F.

Cut the potatoes into chunks and boil them until tender. Drain and mash well. Beat in the milk, salt, and pepper. When smooth, stir in the corn kernels. Set aside.

In a large heavy skillet, heat the oil over medium-high heat. Add the onion, celery, and mushrooms. Sauté until they soften, then add the herbs. Stir in the "hamburger crumbles," soy sauce, and tomato juice and mix well. Spread into a shallow 10-inch round dish or casserole. Top with the potato mixture and spread evenly. Spray with oil from a pump sprayer. Sprinkle with Crumb Topping if using. Bake 30 minutes.

POTATO TOPPING

6 medium russet potatoes, peeled

¼ cup nondairy milk

½ teaspoon salt

⅛ teaspoon white pepper

1 cup canned or cooked frozen or fresh corn kernels

FILLING

1-2 tablespoons extra-virgin olive oil

1 large onion, chopped

¼ cup celery, chopped

¼ pound mushrooms, chopped

¾ teaspoon each dried summer savory and thyme

½ teaspoon crumbled dried sage (not powdered)

Large pinch of celery seed

2 cups vegetarian "hamburger crumbles"

2 tablespoons soy sauce

3 tablespoons tomato juice

Topping (p. 118; optional)

PER SERVING:			
Calories	357	FIBER	8.1g
Total Fat	6g	Carbohydrate	62g
Saturated Fat	1g	Protein	18g
Calories from fat	15%	Sodium	703mg

German-Style Pears and Potatoes

Makes 6 servings

Heat the oil or margarine in a heavy pot. Add the onion and stir to coat with oil. Add flour and cook over low heat, stirring often, until well-browned, 10-15 minutes. Add the broth, brown sugar, and salt and cook over moderate heat, stirring often, to make a smooth sauce. Set aside.

Cut the pears into quarters and core. Cut the potatoes into "fingers" about the same size as the pears. Add to the sauce, cover, and cook over low heat until the potatoes are tender, about 30 minutes. Stir gently a couple of times during the cooking. If it should get too dry and start sticking, add a little water, but don't make the sauce thin. Serve with whole grain bread.

2 tablespoons oil or nondairy margarine

1 medium onion, minced

2 tablespoons flour

1½ cups vegetable broth

1 tablespoon brown sugar

½ teaspoon salt

6 medium pears, washed (peel only if necessary)

4-5 medium thin-skinned potatoes, unpeeled

PER SERVING:			
Calories	258	FIBER	6.9g
Total Fat	5g	Carbohydrate	53g
Saturated Fat	1g	Protein	3g
Calories from fat	17%	Sodium	184mg

POTATO KUGEL

Makes 8 servings

Preheat the oven to 400°F. Lightly oil a 9x13-inch baking pan.

Steam-fry the onions in a large, lightly oiled skillet in vegetable broth until golden and softened. In a large bowl, mix together potatoes, parsley, salt, and pepper. Fold in egg replacer mixture. Smooth the mixture into the prepared pan and bake for 50-60 minutes or until golden.

2 large onions, peeled and grated or minced

3-4 tablespoons vegetable broth

2 pounds russet potatoes, unpeeled, grated

2 tablespoons minced fresh parsley

1 teaspoon salt

Freshly ground black pepper to taste

2 tablespoons powdered egg replacer and ½ cup cold vegetable broth, whisked to a froth

PER SERVING:			
Calories	129	FIBER	3.0g
Total Fat	1g	Carbohydrate	28g
Saturated Fat	0g	Protein	4g
Calories from fat	6%	Sodium	293mg

CAMOTE FRITO
(Peruvian Sweet Potato Chips)

Makes 6 servings

Sweet potatoes are very nutritious, high in fiber and beta carotene, and scrumptious, and they cook more quickly than regular potatoes. They are delicious oven-fried. Sweet potato fries are sold by street vendors in Lima, where my father came from, and other Peruvian towns and cities.

Preheat the oven to 500°F. Cut the sweet potatoes into ⅛-inch thick wedges. Place the "fries" on two nonstick or lightly oiled baking sheets. Bake 5-7 minutes, then turn and bake 5-7 minutes more or until light golden and crispy outside and soft in the middle. Sprinkle with salt and serve hot.

4-6 medium orange-fleshed sweet potatoes, peeled or unpeeled

Coarse salt

PER SERVING:			
Calories	98	FIBER	2.9g
Total Fat	0g	Carbohydrate	23g
Saturated Fat	0g	Protein	2g
Calories from fat	0%	Sodium	10mg

MAINLY GRAINS

Whole grains are neglected in our part of the world, and yet nutritionists tell us that they should make up the bulk of our diet. I think that this neglect is simply a matter of not being familiar with them. I must admit that I have not been very adventurous in the past, preferring rice, corn, oats, and wheat to more unusual grains. As you will notice from the recipes, I love rice! My father, a Peruvian, insisted on long-grain rice every day. But I'm also fond of anything made from corn, of nutty bulghur, and comforting oats. Recently, I've become an aficionado of the South American "ancient grain," quinoa. So you can enjoy the fiber and good nutrition of whole grains whether you are an adventurous cook or a tradition-bound or "comfort zone" cook! (If expense is a consideration, then the more common whole grains will be the cheapest. They are also easiest to find.)

Here are some tips you'll find useful when using whole grains.

LEFTOVER GRAINS can be used in "hash" with leftover vegetables, gravy, and as a meat replacement, as a cereal, or as a crust for savory pies and quiches. Add a cup or so to a recipe for yeast bread (for about 2 loaves).

RESCUING A POT OF BURNED GRAIN: Place a slice of bread on the surface of the grain, cover the pot, and let stand 10 minutes or so. Discard the bread, which should absorb most of the burnt smell. Scrape the grain out of the pot, being careful not to disturb the burned portion on the bottom.

REHEATING RICE AND OTHER GRAINS: Place the grain in a heat-proof bowl, or a sieve, colander, or steamer. Place about 2 inches above simmering water in a pot. Cover and steam 10 minutes. Or, place the grain in a microwave-proof bowl, cover with waxed paper and microwave on high for about 2 minutes for 1-2 cups.

PILAFS WITH OTHER WHOLE GRAINS: When I use the term "toasted" below, I mean that the raw grain has been stir-fried in a heavy, hot, dry skillet for 3-5 minutes. This is very important for some grains, resulting in a more flavorful and dry, fluffy pilaf. Quinoa makes a particularly delightful pilaf and is especially delicious with some corn kernels added.

Follow the basic directions for Basic Pilaf (page 146) substituting one of the following:

➤ 2 cups amaranth and 2 cups broth. Cook 7 minutes; let stand 10 minutes.

➤ 2 cups toasted millet and 4 cups broth. Cook 20 minutes; let stand 5-10 minutes.

➤ 2 cups toasted steel-cut or scotch oats and 3 cups broth. Cook 12 minutes; let stand 10 minutes.

➤ 2 cups toasted quinoa and 4 cups broth. Cook 15-20 minutes; let stand 5-10 minutes.

BASIC PILAF

Makes 6-8 servings

Pilaf is a delicious grain dish cooked in broth. It's usually made with rice and/or bulghur, but check out the directions for making it with other grains (below). If you want to use just bulghur, use 4 cups broth. If you want to use just rice, use 3 cups broth.

In a large saucepan with a tight-fitting lid, heat the oil over high heat. Add the onion and celery and stir-fry until the onion starts to soften. Add the bulghur, rice, herbs, and any optionals, and stir-fry 1 minute. Add the broth and salt and bring to a boil. Reduce heat to low and cook, covered, 20 minutes. Let stand 5 minutes. Fluff with a fork before serving.

TURKISH PILAF: Add chopped green onions and dried currants or raisins. One to two tablespoons lemon juice and perhaps the grated zest of 1 lemon is also tasty in a pilaf.

I tablespoon extra-virgin olive oil

I large onion, chopped

I cup celery, chopped

I cup bulghur

I cup quick-cooking brown rice

I teaspoon dried rosemary, crushed, or dried thyme or oregano

½ teaspoon curry powder or ground coriander (optional)

¼ cup minced fresh parsley (optional)

4 cups vegetable broth

Salt to taste

VARIATIONS

1) Other additions might be minced garlic; 1 cup frozen whole small green beans, thawed and sliced; 1 cup cubed or grated summer squash; 1 cup corn kernels; some chopped red or green bell pepper, 1 cup chopped broccoli or other vegetables or a mixture; 1 chopped apple and ½ teaspoon cinnamon.

2) Add ¼ pound chopped mushrooms or a chopped or shredded carrot to the onion and celery.

3) Add 1-2 tablespoons toasted sesame seeds, sunflower seeds or almonds.

4) For a more substantial dish, add chopped vegetarian "sausage" or other meat replacement.

PER SERVING:			
Calories	135	FIBER	4.1g
Total Fat	3g	Carbohydrate	25g
Saturated Fat	0g	Protein	4g
Calories from fat	20%	Sodium	22mg

MY BASIC BROWN RICE COOKING FORMULA

Most rice recipes call for too much liquid. I use 1½ cups liquid for every 1 cup dry rice, no matter what kind of rice or how much. I do pour long grain rice slowly into boiling water or broth (to make the grains more separate), but I start short grain rice in cold water.

Use a heavy-bottomed pot with a tight lid. Bring the rice to a boil, then cover it tightly and turn down to a low simmer, 45 minutes. Turn the heat off and leave the pot tightly covered until you are ready to serve it. Long grain rice should be fluffed with a fork before serving.

Presoaking brown rice (any kind) in its measured cooking water for AT LEAST 4 hours before cooking will allow you to reduce the cooking time to 25 minutes.

If you like very dry, fluffy rice, follow the directions above, using any long grain brown rice. Bring it to a boil with the water. Have the oven preheated to 350 to 400°F. Use an oven-and-stovetop-safe pot, such as cast iron. Cover the pot, place it in the oven, and bake for 45 minutes.

DO NOT cook brown rice in tomato juice or with other acid products (such as fruit juices, dried fruits, etc. They harden the bran on the outside of the rice and makes it take much longer to cook. If you want tomato, fruit, lemon, etc., in your brown rice, cook the rice first, then add the acid ingredient and simmer gently until the rice absorbs some of it. (See the Jambalaya recipe on page 160 for an example of this.)

QUICK CURRIED RICE

Makes 4-6 servings

This versatile dish is a good way to use leftover rice, and it makes a great stuffing for squash and other vegetables, too.

In a large nonstick or lightly oiled skillet, steam-fry the onions, celery, mushrooms and peas, if using. Add the garam masala and stir-fry 1 minute. Add all of the remaining ingredients and stir-fry until hot.

4 medium onions, minced

3 stalks celery, sliced

I cup sliced mushrooms (optional)

I cup frozen peas (optional)

I teaspoon garam masala or curry powder or more to taste

½ cup raisins or dried currants

4 cups cooked long-grain brown rice or brown basmati rice or other cooked whole grain

½ teaspoon salt

Pepper to taste

PER SERVING:			
Calories	269	FIBER	6.5g
Total Fat	2g	Carbohydrate	59g
Saturated Fat	0g	Protein	6g
Calories from fat	6%	Sodium	250mg

FRIED BROWN RICE
Basic Chinese-Style

Makes 6 servings

Rice is normally eaten plain in China, but occasionally a savory or fried rice dish will be made with leftover rice and other ingredients. Fried Rice doesn't need to be oily, and it should be seasoned with salt or just a little light soy sauce. Use the suggestions I have made in the recipe, or change it to suit what you have on hand. In China, this would be made with white rice, but cooked long-grain brown rice makes an excellent dish. Start with cold leftover rice.

1½ tablespoons oil

1 cup shredded commercial flavored baked tofu or slivered vegetarian "ham" or "Canadian back bacon"

1½ cups fresh mung bean sprouts or finely shredded Napa or Savoy cabbage or a mixture

½ large green or red bell pepper, chopped OR ½ cup frozen baby peas, thawed, OR frozen peas and carrots, thawed

1 cup sliced mushrooms, zucchini, cucumber, or shredded lettuce (optional)

2 large green onions, chopped

4 cups cold cooked long-grain brown rice

½ tablespoon toasted sesame oil

Salt and pepper to taste

Heat a large heavy wok or nonstick stir-fry pan or sauté pan over high heat. Add the oil. When the oil is hot, add the tofu and the vegetables. Stir-fry several minutes or until the cabbage starts to wilt. Add the rice, breaking up the clumps with your fingers. Add the sesame oil and salt and pepper, and keep turning the rice with a spatula until the rice is hot and everything is well-mixed. Taste for salt and pepper and serve immediately.

VARIATION: Substitute any other cooked whole grain for the rice.

PER SERVING:			
Calories	260	FIBER	4.2g
Total Fat	9g	Carbohydrate	35g
Saturated Fat	1g	Protein	11g
Calories from fat	31%	Sodium	15mg

GOLDEN OATS PILAF

Makes 4 servings

This is an unusual and delicious, savory way to use oatmeal, which is high in insoluble fiber. It cooks very quickly and makes an interesting change from rice, pasta, or other grains. (It would also make an interesting stuffing.)

In a blender, combine the flaxseeds and water and blend several minutes. Place the oatmeal in a medium bowl and add the flaxseed mixture; stir to coat thoroughly. Heat the oil in a large heavy skillet over medium heat. Add the oats mixture and stir constantly 3 minutes or until the oats are dry, separated, and lightly browned. Add the broth and salt. Cook, covered, 2-3 minutes or until the liquid evaporates, stirring 2-3 times. Serve immediately.

¼ cup water

1 tablespoon flaxseeds

1½ cups rolled oats

1 tablespoon extra-virgin olive oil
or nondairy margarine

¾ cup water, vegetarian broth, or juice

¼ teaspoon salt

VARIATIONS

1) Add any or all of the following: chopped, sautéed onion and/or garlic, ¼ cup chopped fresh parsley, and ½-1 teaspoon of your favorite dried herb (or ½-1 tablespoon fresh, chopped).

2) You can also add one of the following:

1 medium ripe tomato, chopped

1 tablespoon soy "bacon" chips or bits

¼ cup chopped vegetarian "Canadian
back bacon" or "ham"

¾ cup sautéed mushroom slices

2 tablespoons chopped green onion

½ cup sautéed chopped
bell pepper (any color)

1 cup steamed chopped broccoli

1 cup thinly sliced zucchini,
steamed crisp-tender

PER SERVING:			
Calories	158	FIBER	3.7g
Total Fat	6g	Carbohydrate	0g
Saturated Fat	1g	Protein	5g
Calories from fat	34%	Sodium	134mg

TRIGO
Wheat Kernel Pilaf, Lima-Style

Makes 6 servings

This unusual Peruvian dish, made with whole wheat kernels, or wheat berries, was given to me by my cousin Charo. She just gave me an idea of the ingredients, and I consulted an old, badly translated Peruvian cookbook of my mother's for more help. This is what I came up with, and I like it very much! Charo insists that the wheat kernels we get here are not the same as the "trigo" they have in Peru, but I made it with cooked soft wheat berries, and it tasted fine to me! If you like savory foods for breakfast, the leftovers are delicious in the morning!

1 tablespoon extra-virgin olive oil

Few drops toasted sesame oil (optional)

½ cup chopped onions

2 cloves garlic, crushed

2 medium, ripe tomatoes, chopped

½ tablespoon dried red pepper flakes

1¼ cup cooked wheat berries (hard or soft; reserve cooking water)

1 pound Yukon Gold potatoes, unpeeled, cooked and cubed

½ cup grated nondairy mozzarella cheese

¼ cup chopped parsley

Salt and freshly ground black pepper to taste

Heat the oil in a large nonstick skillet. Sauté the onions until softened. Add the garlic, tomatoes, and pepper flakes; sauté several minutes. This is what Latins call a "sofrito." Add the cooked wheat and potatoes and cook, stirring occasionally, several minutes. Add some of the wheat cooking water if it's too dry. Stir in the cheese and parsley, and taste for salt and pepper. Serve immediately.

TIP: To cook wheat berries, soak them overnight in 4 cups water. Cook in the soaking water 50-60 minutes or until tender.

PER SERVING:			
Calories	164	FIBER	4.2g
Total Fat	4g	Carbohydrate	30g
Saturated Fat	0g	Protein	5g
Calories from fat	21%	Sodium	40mg

HERBED VEGETABLE AND BULGHUR SKILLET

Makes 2-4 servings

I've always loved bulghur—it's nutty-tasting and cooks quickly. This dish is colorful, smells and tastes heavenly, and is ready in less than 30 minutes—a complete meal in one dish! You can substitute other vegetables for the broccoli, if you like. This dish is quite moist when made with ¾ cup bulghur. If you prefer a drier dish, use 1 cup bulghur.

In a 12-inch skillet, heat 1½ tablespoons of the oil over medium-high heat. Add the vegetarian chicken and cook until brown. Remove from the pan and add the remaining ½ tablespoon oil to the pan. When it is hot, add the celery, carrot, onion, mushrooms, and garlic and sauté until the onion is softened, adding a few drops of water if necessary to prevent sticking.

Add the bulghur and stir around briefly, then add the herbs and broth. Cover, reduce the heat to low and cook 10 minutes. Add the browned vegetarian chicken and broccoli, cover, and cook 10 minutes more. Add pepper and fluff the mixture with a spoon, mixing the ingredients together. Serve immediately.

2 tablespoons extra-virgin olive oil

1½-2 cups cubed vegetarian chicken or savory baked tofu

½ cup chopped celery

½ cup diced unpeeled carrot

½ cup chopped onion

4 large mushrooms, sliced

2 cloves garlic, chopped

¾-1 cup bulghur

1 teaspoon of your favorite dried herb, such as thyme, rosemary, basil, or oregano (or 1 tablespoon chopped fresh)

2 cups chicken-style vegetarian broth

¾ pound fresh broccoli, cut into small florets

Freshly ground black pepper to taste

PER SERVING:			
Calories	442	FIBER	13.4g
Total Fat	23g	Carbohydrate	39g
Saturated Fat	3g	Protein	31g
Calories from fat	46%	Sodium	84mg

KUSHERIE
Egyptian Rice, Lentil, Macaroni with Spicy Tomato Sauce

Makes 8 servings

Serve with a salad or steamed vegetables. Start the rice and lentils and make the sauce and browned onions while they are cooking.

To cook the rice and lentils, lightly oil a heavy pot with olive oil and add the lentils. Stir over high heat until they start to change color; add all of the remaining ingredients. Cover and bring to a boil. Reduce heat to low; simmer 60 minutes.

To make the sauce, combine all the sauce ingredients in a medium saucepan and bring to a boil over high heat. Reduce heat and simmer, uncovered, 20-30 minutes.

To make the browned onions, heat the olive oil in a large skillet over medium-high heat. Add the onions and garlic and stir-fry until they are soft and browned, adding a few drops of water if necessary to prevent sticking.

Mix the cooked, drained macaroni with ¼ cup of the sauce.

Serve the rice and lentils side-by-side with the macaroni, all topped by the sauce and browned onions. You can also top this with nondairy sour cream or soy yogurt.

RICE AND LENTILS
Olive oil

1¼ cup dried brown lentils

1½ cup long-grain brown basmati rice

4 cups water

4 vegetarian bouillon cubes

Pepper to taste

2 cups dry whole wheat macaroni, cooked separately and drained

SPICY TOMATO SAUCE
3½ cups tomato juice

1 (6-ounce) can tomato paste (¾ cup)

1 green pepper, seeded and chopped

3 tablespoons chopped celery leaves

3 cloves garlic, chopped

1 tablespoon sugar

1½ teaspoon ground cumin

1 teaspoon salt

¼ teaspoon cayenne pepper or to taste

BROWNED ONIONS
2 tablespoons extra-virgin olive oil

3 large onions, sliced

4 cloves garlic, minced

PER SERVING:			
Calories	361	FIBER	13.7g
Total Fat	5g	Carbohydrate	69g
Saturated Fat	1g	Protein	15g
Calories from fat	12%	Sodium	762mg

Arabic "Pizzas"

Makes 6 servings

These are often called Arabic, Lebanese, or Armenian meat pies because they are basically pita bread dough baked with a topping of minced meat, tomatoes, and herbs. Here, the topping is made with vegetarian "burger" instead of meat and is baked on top of purchased (or your own homemade) soft whole wheat pita breads for ease and convenience—and they are delicious! These make a great light lunch, and deserve to be as popular as hummus and falafel.

1 small onion, minced

Oil

1½ cup commercial vegetarian "hamburger crumbles"

½ cup chopped canned tomatoes, drained

¼ cup chopped minced parsley

1 tablespoon ground flaxseeds

1 teaspoon lemon juice

½ teaspoon ground cumin

¼ teaspoon salt

Red pepper sauce and black pepper to taste

Nondairy sour cream or soy yogurt

6 fresh soft whole wheat pita breads

Preheat the oven to 400°F.

Sauté the onion with a little oil or tomato juice drained from the canned tomatoes over high heat in a large nonstick skillet until softened. Mix in all of the remaining ingredients except the pita bread. Cook, stirring, until mixed well and heated through. Divide the burger mixture equally among the breads and spread evenly. Place on unoiled baking sheets. Bake 10 minutes, or until the bottoms are slightly crispy. Serve hot or at room temperature with sour cream or soy yogurt to spread on top.

PER SERVING:

Calories	223	FIBER	6.7g
Total Fat	2g	Carbohydrate	41g
Saturated Fat	0g	Protein	12g
Calories from fat	8%	Sodium	466mg

WALNUT FETTUCINE
Whole Grain Fettucine or Linguine with Italian Walnut Creme Sauce

Makes 4 servings

I think creamy sauces suit whole wheat pasta better than tomato sauces. This is a modern, lighter version of a very old Italian recipe. The sauce is very simple to make and is excellent on whole grain pasta.

1 pound whole wheat linguine or fettucine, cooked until al dente and drained

WALNUT CREME SAUCE

¾ cup chopped walnuts

2 cups nondairy milk

1 vegetarian chicken-style bouillon cube, crumbled

1 small clove garlic, crushed

2 tablespoons nondairy Parmesan cheese

Salt to taste

1-2 teaspoons chopped fresh marjoram (optional)

¼ teaspoon freshly ground nutmeg

Heat a cast-iron skillet, or other heavy pan, over high heat. Add the walnuts and reduce the heat to medium. Toast the walnuts, stirring frequently and watching them constantly, until they turn color and smell toasty. Remove them from the pan and process until almost ground to a paste.

Combine the milk, bouillon cube, garlic, and walnuts in a heavy medium-sized saucepan or sauté pan. Bring to a boil over medium-high heat and keep at a low boil until it has reduced somewhat and thickened to a sauce. Remove from the heat and add the optional marjoram, and the nutmeg and soy Parmesan. Taste for salt. Serve immediately over linguine with additional Parmesan if desired. Traditionally, no pepper is used in this sauce.

PER SERVING:			
Calories	325	FIBER	7.6g
Total Fat	17g	Carbohydrate	36g
Saturated Fat	2g	Protein	13g
Calories from fat	47%	Sodium	20mg

CORIANDER RICE
with Peas, Peruvian-Style

Makes 6 servings

This delicious rice dish, a variation of the Peruvian dish Arroz con Pato, *makes a great side dish or light main dish.*

In a heavy medium pot with a tight-fitting lid, bring the water to a boil with the bouillon cubes. Add the rice and bring to a boil. Reduce heat, cover, and simmer 45-60 minutes or until the rice is tender; set aside.

To make the sofrito, heat the oils over medium-high heat in a large nonstick skillet with a tight-fitting lid, and sauté the onion, jalapeño, garlic, and red bell pepper, if using, until garlic begins to brown slightly. Add the cilantro, coriander, and cumin, and stir-fry 1 minute.

Add the cooked rice, beer, peas, and pepper, and 1 optional ingredient if using. Bring to a boil, cover, and cook 15-20 minutes, or until the beer is absorbed. Taste for salt and pepper.

PER SERVING:			
Calories	315	FIBER	6.2g
Total Fat	6g	Carbohydrate	56g
Saturated Fat	1g	Protein	8g
Calories from fat	17%	Sodium	289mg

RICE

3⅓ cups boiling water

4 vegetarian bouillon cubes

2 cups brown basmati rice

SOFRITO

1-2 tablespoons extra-virgin olive oil

1 teaspoon toasted sesame oil

1 large onion, minced

2 tablespoons minced pickled or canned jalapeño

6 large cloves garlic, minced

1 red bell pepper, seeded and diced (optional)

2 tablespoons minced fresh cilantro (or 1 tablespoon dried)

1 tablespoon ground coriander

1 teaspoon ground cumin

1 cup dark beer, ale, or stout (can be nonalcoholic)

1 cup frozen baby peas (petit pois)

Freshly ground pepper to taste

OPTIONAL (USE ONE)

1 (15-ounce) can (or 1½ cups cooked) chickpeas, rinsed and drained

1½ cups corn kernels

2 cups commercial savory baked tofu or tempeh, cubed and browned

BULGHUR BURGERS

Makes 12 patties

These simple patties are a gourmet experience. They're also good cold!

Soak the bulghur in the water in a large bowl until water is absorbed, about 10-15 minutes. Preheat oven to 400°F.

Add all of the remaining ingredients to the bulghur, mix well, and shape into 12 thin patties. Bake on a lightly oiled baking sheet covered with foil, until golden brown, about 10 minutes; turn and bake, uncovered, until other side is golden brown, about 10 minutes more. Or, cook in a nonstick skillet, covered, over medium heat until browned, about 5-7 minutes; turn, uncover, and cook until other side is browned. Serve with gravy or any other sauce you prefer.

¾ cup bulghur

¾ cup boiling water

1 minced or grated onion
(or 1 cup minced green onion)

1 unpeeled potato, grated,
or a mixture of grated potato
and grated unpeeled carrot

2 tablespoons tomato sauce or ketchup

2 tablespoons ground flaxseeds

1 tablespoon soy sauce

2 cloves garlic, pressed

½ teaspoon each dried thyme and
marjoram (or ½ tablespoon each
chopped fresh)

½ teaspoon paprika

1 cup fine fresh whole wheat
breadcrumbs

2 tablespoons pure gluten powder

2 tablespoons parsley (optional)

PER SERVING:			
Calories	54	FIBER	2g
Total Fat	1g	Carbohydrate	10g
Saturated Fat	0g	Protein	2g
Calories from fat	16%	Sodium	115mg

Savory Mushroom Patties

Makes 12 patties

This is another deceptively simple recipe that is utterly delicious! Try cremini or portobello mushrooms.

In a large bowl, mix the breadcrumbs, oats, gluten flour, and herbs. Add all of the remaining ingredients. Mix well and form into 12 thin patties. Cook on a non-stick skillet, covered, over medium heat about 7 minutes; turn, uncover, and cook 7 minutes more. Or, bake, covered, on a lightly oiled cookie sheet at 400°F until golden brown, about 10 minutes; turn, uncover, and cook 10 minutes more. Serve with gravy or any other sauce you prefer.

1½ cups fresh whole wheat breadcrumbs

6 tablespoons quick-cooking rolled oats

3 tablespoons pure gluten powder

½ teaspoon each dried marjoram, oregano, and thyme OR
½ tablespoon each chopped fresh

½ teaspoon paprika

1 tablespoon soy sauce
or 1 teaspoon salt

2 cups minced fresh mushrooms

2 cups minced onions

1 cup minced celery

4 cloves garlic, pressed

2 tablespoons minced fresh parsley

2 tablespoons ground flaxseeds

PER SERVING:			
Calories	48	FIBER	1.6g
Total Fat	1g	Carbohydrate	8g
Saturated Fat	0g	Protein	3g
Calories from fat	18%	Sodium	110mg

Carrot-Oat Patties

Maks 10 patties

A food processor makes this recipe very easy to assemble; otherwise, you can hand-grate the onions and carrots fairly quickly. They are also excellent cold.

2 large onions, minced or coarsely grated
1 cup quick-cooking rolled oats
1 cup fine fresh whole grain breadcrumbs
¼ cup soy flour or chickpea flour
1-2 tablespoons tahini or other nut butter
1 teaspoon salt
½ teaspoon each dried thyme, crumbled sage, marjoram, and garlic granules
¾ cup grated carrots
¼ cup minced toasted walnuts
⅓ cup hot water
1 tablespoon soy sauce

In a lightly oiled nonstick skillet, stir-fry the onions over high heat until soft, adding a few drops of water as necessary to prevent sticking. In a large bowl, mix the oats, breadcrumbs, flour, tahini, salt, and herbs. Add the onions, carrots, walnuts, hot water, and soy sauce.

Mix the ingredients well and form into 10 thin patties. Cook the patties in a lightly oiled nonstick skillet, covered, over medium-low heat for 4-5 minutes; turn and cook, uncovered, 4-5 minutes more. Serve hot with ketchup or gravy.

PER SERVING:

Calories	96	FIBER	2.7g
Total Fat	4g	Carbohydrate	12g
Saturated Fat	1g	Protein	4g
Calories from fat	37%	Sodium	325mg

Zucchini "Sausage" Patties

Makes 10 patties

These are very tasty all on their own, hot or cold. They would make a nice brunch dish.

Mix the rice, water, and pinch of salt in a small saucepan with a tight-fitting lid. Bring to a boil, reduce heat to low, cover and cook 45 minutes.

Meanwhile, mix the shredded zucchini and coarse salt in a sieve or colander; set aside to drain while rice cooks.

Transfer the cooked rice to a bowl. Rinse the zucchini well to wash off the salt, and squeeze it dry in a clean tea towel.

Heat the oil in a nonstick skillet. Add the chopped "ham" and brown a bit. Add the zucchini and garlic and sauté briefly. Add to the rice with all of the remaining ingredients. Mix well. Chill the mixture for 2 hours or more. Form into 10 patties. Cook on an indoor grill for about 7 minutes. Or, fry on both sides over medium heat with a little olive oil. Or, dredge in breadcrumbs and fry in oil.

¾ cup short-grain brown rice

1⅛ cups water

Pinch of salt

2 pounds zucchini, shredded

2 tablespoons coarse salt*

1 tablespoon olive oil

4 ounces vegetarian "ham" or "Canadian back bacon," chopped fine

1 tablespoon minced or crushed garlic

½ cup firm tofu, well-mashed

1 tablespoon lemon juice

1 tablespoon nutritional yeast

1 tablespoon minced fresh basil (or 1 teaspoon dried)

½ tablespoon minced fresh marjoram (or ½ teaspoon dried)

½-1 teaspoon salt

Freshly ground black pepper to taste

*This gets washed away, so don't be concerned.

PER SERVING:			
Calories	121	FIBER	2g
Total Fat	6g	Carbohydrate	12g
Saturated Fat	1g	Protein	6g
Calories from fat	44%	Sodium	429mg

VEGETARIAN JAMBALAYA

Makes 8 servings

A different cooking method ensures success with brown rice in this innovative recipe.

In a medium-heavy saucepan, bring the rice, water, and salt to a boil. Cover, reduce heat, and simmer on low for 45 minutes. (This can be done ahead of time.)

Brown "sausages" and tofu in large skillet in the sesame oil; remove and set aside.

To make the Seasoning Mixture, in the same skillet, heat the remaining olive oil and sesame oil. Add the onions and cook over medium heat until they start to soften. Add the garlic, celery, and bell peppers. Cook until they wilt a bit. Add the herbs and spices and cook for a few minutes. Add the vegetarian "bacon" or "ham," tofu, and browned "sausage"; stir well. Add the tomatoes and cook for a few minutes. Add the broth and cooked rice and mix thoroughly. Cover and cook on low until rice is heated through and liquids are absorbed, about 15 minutes. Stir in green onions and parsley and serve.

1½ cups brown basmati rice

2½ cups water

1 teaspoon salt

1 package vegetarian plain or Italian "sausages" or vegetarian "chorizo" or 2 vegetarian jumbo "weiners" (or 4 small ones), sliced

1½ cups cut-up commercial flavored, baked tofu or deep-fried tofu

1 tablespoon toasted sesame oil

SEASONING MIXTURE

1½ tablespoons olive oil

½ tablespoon toasted sesame oil

2 onions, chopped

4 cloves garlic, minced

½ cup celery, chopped

1 medium green bell pepper, chopped

1 medium red bell pepper, chopped

2 bay leaves, crushed

1 teaspoon paprika

1 teaspoon dried basil

1 teaspoon dried thyme

½ teaspoon freshly ground black pepper

½ teaspoon cayenne pepper

½ teaspoon chili powder

½ teaspoon salt

⅛ teaspoon allspice

⅛ teaspoon ground cloves

½ cup sliced vegetarian "Canadian back bacon" or "ham" or 1 tablespoon soy "bacon" chips or bits

1 cup canned diced tomatoes with juice or chopped juicy fresh tomatoes

¾ cup vegetable broth

4 green onions, chopped

3 tablespoons minced parsley

PER SERVING:

Calories	307	FIBER	5.8g
Total Fat	14g	Carbohydrate	31g
Saturated Fat	2g	Protein	16g
Calories from fat	41%	Sodium	712mg

NUTTY "CHEESE" BALLS

Makes 20 "meatballs"

Wait until serving before topping them with tomato sauce and nondairy Parmesan cheese so that they don't fall apart.

Preheat the oven to 350°F. Oil a baking sheet.

Combine all of the ingredients well, using your hands, if necessary. Form into 20 balls and place on the baking sheet. Spray the balls with oil from a pump sprayer. Bake 15 minutes. Turn and bake 15 minutes more.

¼ medium-large onion, finely minced

2 sprigs parsley, finely minced

1 clove garlic, crushed

⅔ cup crumbled, drained medium-firm tofu (not silken)

1 tablespoon light miso

1 tablespoon tahini

¼ cup nutritional yeast flakes

1 tablespoon pure gluten powder

½ teaspoon salt

¼ teaspoon white pepper

1 cup (packed down a bit) finely ground soft fresh whole grain breadcrumbs*

¾ cup walnut pieces, minced or ground

*Use a light-textured whole grain bread, not a dark, heavy one.

COOKING NOTE: It's easy to make this recipe in a food processor. First, mince the nuts and set aside. Grind the breadcrumbs and set aside. Add the onion (peeled and cut into chunks) and parsley and process until finely minced. Add the tofu, garlic, miso, tahini, yeast, gluten powder, salt, and pepper and process briefly. Finally, add the breadcrumbs and nuts and process again. (No need to wash the processor bowl in between steps.)

PER SERVING:

Calories	54	FIBER	0.7g
Total Fat	4g	Carbohydrate	3g
Saturated Fat	0g	Protein	3g
Calories from fat	66%	Sodium	84mg

CHILES RELLENOS CASSEROLE

Makes 6-8 servings

This is a great potluck dish!

Preheat the oven to 350°F.

In a large, heavy skillet, heat the oil over medium-high heat. Sauté the onions and garlic until they start to soften. Add the "hamburger crumbles" and taco seasoning. Stir-fry 2 minutes. Set aside. Mash the drained tofu in a bowl with the nondairy milk and the salt. Set aside.

Drain the canned chiles and slit them open on one side. Cut them lengthwise into quarters. Arrange ½ of the chile quarters in an oiled 9 x 13-inch baking pan. Top with the rice, then the "hamburger" mixture, then the mashed tofu mixture, then the corn kernels, and, lastly, the beans (you can just arrange dabs of this over the corn—it's hard to spread it). Arrange the rest of the chile quarters over this, then top with the Bechamel Sauce, spreading evenly.

Sprinkle the top with chili powder and arrange red and green bell peppers and olives on top for garnish, if desired. Bake 65 minutes. Let stand 5 minutes before serving.

2 tablespoons extra-virgin olive oil

2 onions, chopped

2 large garlic cloves, minced

2 cups vegetarian "hamburger crumbles"

2 tablespoons taco seasoning

1 pound medium-firm tofu

6 tablespoons nondairy milk

½ teaspoon salt

1 (27-ounce) can whole green (California) chiles

3 cups cooked long-grain brown rice

2 cups corn kernels, drained

2 cups canned or homemade vegetarian "refried beans" (p. 108) or Spicy Mexican Bean Dip (p. 62)

1 recipe medium-thick Bechamel Sauce (p. 84)

Chili powder, red or green bell pepper slices, sliced black olives (optional)

PER SERVING:			
Calories	505	FIBER	16.3g
Total Fat	17g	Carbohydrate	67g
Saturated Fat	3g	Protein	27g
Calories from fat	30%	Sodium	808mg

DESSERTS

If you think "delicious high-fiber desserts" is an oxymoron, I'm going to set about proving you wrong! We've come a long way since the 1960s and '70s in terms of baking with whole grains. Desserts made with whole grain flours and natural fruits don't have to be heavy and brown! Once you know the tricks, it's easy to make your desserts count in terms of nutrition, and yet you don't have to be aware of that with every bite. Not only that, but it isn't necessary to pack fat into desserts to make them tender. So enjoy this sampling of 21st century healthful desserts.

ADDING FIBER AND LOWERING FAT

The first step in adding fiber to desserts is to use whole grain flours and whole grains, such as rolled oats. The bran of wheat, oats, and rice can also be added to many desserts for extra fiber. The best candidates for high-fiber conversions are fruity desserts and things like spice cakes—these types of desserts are not expected to look white. I personally don't care for most chocolate cakes made from whole wheat flour, but I have a recipe for high-fiber brownies that is a winner!

Nuts and seeds, including ground flaxseeds, though used judiciously because of their high fat content, also provide fiber. Fruits, fresh and dried, and vegetables add fiber to desserts as well. Berries are a particularly excellent source of fiber (and antioxidants), so I use them frequently. Apples contain lots of soluble fiber in the form of pectin, especially in the peel. Winter squash, such as pumpkin, carrots, and sweet potatoes are sweet, high-fiber vegetables often used in desserts.

LOWERING THE FAT

Because the gluten in wheat becomes tough in baking if not coated with fat, low-fat baked goods should be made with at least half pastry flour (preferably whole wheat), which has less gluten than all-purpose flour. You may prefer to use all pastry flour. Or, experiment with half wheat flour and half low-gluten or nongluten grain flours, such as oat, barley, rice, etc. An additional way to avoid toughening the gluten is to mix low-fat batters gently, the same method as for mixing muffin batters.

Smooth, unsweetened applesauce is a great oil replacer in baked goods. Use it to replace ⅔-¾ of the oil called for in recipes. (This doesn't make as good a replacement for solid fats.) Plus, it's one more source of fiber. It's light in color and the flavor is not assertive. You can also use other fruit purées, such as puréed cooked prunes or dried apricots (or baby-food prunes or apricots), prune butter, apple butter, and even puréed pumpkin or other squash.

WHOLE WHEAT OIL PASTRY

Makes 8 servings

This recipe makes a light and tender crust with half whole wheat flour and half the fat of ordinary pastry. Pure (rather than extra-virgin) olive oil makes an excellent baking fat.

Mix the dry ingredients in a bowl. In a smaller bowl, whisk the nondairy milk-lemon juice mixture with the oil. Quickly stir the liquid mixture into the dry ingredients and mix briefly, forming the pastry into a ball. If it's too dry, add cold water a few drops at a time until it holds together. Don't overmix or the pastry will be tough.

If made ahead of time, place dough in a plastic bag and refrigerate for several hours up to several days. To bake unfilled shells, prick the bottom and sides with a fork and bake 8-10 minutes at 425°F.

SWEET VARIATION: Use 2-4 tablespoons sugar. Add ½ teaspoon lemon extract and ¼ teaspoon vanilla to liquid ingredients. For 2 crusts, use ¼ to ½ cup finely ground unbleached sugar, 1 teaspoon pure lemon extract, and ½ teaspoon vanilla.

ONE 9- OR 10-INCH CRUST

½ cup minus 1 tablespoon white cake or pastry flour plus ½ cup whole wheat flour OR ½ cup minus 1 tablespoon whole wheat pastry flour plus ½ cup unbleached white flour*

⅜ teaspoon each baking powder, sugar, and salt

3 tablespoons nondairy milk mixed with ½ teaspoon lemon juice

3 tablespoons pure olive oil

TWO 9- OR 10-INCH CRUSTS

⅞ cup white cake or pastry flour plus 1 cup whole wheat flour OR ⅞ cup whole wheat pastry flour plus 1 cup unbleached white flour

¾ teaspoon each baking powder, sugar, and salt

6 tablespoons nondairy milk mixed with 1 teaspoon lemon juice

6 tablespoons pure olive oil

*NOTE: It is important to use half pastry flour.

PER SERVING:			
Calories	99	FIBER	1.2g
Total Fat	5g	Carbohydrate	10g
Saturated Fat	1g	Protein	2g
Calories from fat	45%	Sodium	116mg

ITALIAN-STYLE APPLE TART

Makes 8 servings

This delicious tart is very popular during winter months in Italy, as I'm sure it will be in your home.

Preheat the oven to 350°F.

Roll out the dough to fit a 10-inch tart or pie pan. (If using a pie pan, bring the pastry up to the inside top of the pan, and flute it to make a shallow shell—not over the edge like an American pie.) Trim the top edge. Neatly prick the bottom and sides with a fork and bake 5 minutes. Cool on a rack. Do not turn the oven off.

Mix in the cinnamon, if using, with the applesauce and spread it over the cooled crust. Arrange the apple slices on the applesauce, overlapping them in concentric circles. Brush the apples with nondairy milk. Bake 25-30 minutes.

Meanwhile, combine the preserves and lemon juice in a small saucepan and bring to a boil. Strain through a fine-mesh sieve. While still hot, brush glaze over the apples. Cool before serving. Serve with your favorite nondairy topping.

1 Whole Wheat Oil Pastry crust sweet variation (p. 164)

¾ cup thick lightly sweetened applesauce

Pinch of ground cinnamon (optional)

3 large tart apples, peeled, cored, and thinly sliced

Nondairy milk for brushing

½ cup apricot preserves (preferably fruit-sweetened)

2 tablespoons fresh lemon juice

PER SERVING:			
Calories	204	FIBER	3.8g
Total Fat	6g	Carbohydrate	36g
Saturated Fat	1g	Protein	2g
Calories from fat	26%	Sodium	117mg

FRENCH STRAWBERRY PIE

Makes 8 servings

Berries are full of fiber, so any dessert featuring berries is a bonus! This pie should be served soon after assembling, so that the crust doesn't get soggy. This has been a favorite in my family for many years.

Mix the Filling ingredients together well and set aside in the refrigerator.

To make the Glaze, bring the chopped strawberries, water, syrup, and salt to a boil in a medium saucepan and boil hard 2 minutes; strain. Return to pan and add the cornstarch mixture. Stir over high heat until thickened. Cool.

Just before serving, spread filling in cooled crust. Arrange the large whole trimmed berries attractively on top of the filling, pointy ends up. Pour cooled glaze over berries. Garnish with whipped topping. Serve immediately.

FILLING

2 cups nondairy cream cheese

1½ tablespoons maple syrup or fruit concentrate syrup

½ teaspoon vanilla

GLAZE

2 cups strawberries, chopped

¾ cup water

⅓ cup maple syrup or fruit concentrate syrup

Dash of salt

2 tablespoons cornstarch mixed with 1½ tablespoons water

1 baked 9-inch Whole Wheat Oil Pastry crust (p. 164)

Large whole, unblemished strawberries (trimmed) to cover the bottom of the crust

Nondairy whipped topping

PER SERVING:			
Calories	340	FIBER	3g
Total Fat	21g	Carbohydrate	35g
Saturated Fat	6g	Protein	4g
Calories from fat	55%	Sodium	298mg

STRAWBERRY SORBET

Makes 4 servings

*Strawberries make a delicious
frozen dessert that's surprisingly
high in fiber.*

Purée the strawberries with the lemon
juice in a food processor or blender. In a
stainless steel saucepan over high heat,
heat the sugar and water, stirring constantly, until the sugar is dissolved.
Combine with the strawberries and wine.
Chill and freeze according to the directions with your machine.

VARIATIONS: Substitute other berries for
the strawberries. Or you can substitute
fresh orange juice or ½ cup water plus ¼
cup marsala or sherry for the water.

NOTE: Alcohol keeps the sorbet from
freezing rock-hard, so if you don't use
wine or hard cider, soak 1 teaspoon vegetarian kosher gelatin, ¼ teaspoon powdered agar, or 1½ teaspoons agar flakes
in 1 tablespoon water and add to the hot
sugar mixture.

2 pints fresh strawberries, sliced

1 tablespoon lemon juice

¾ cup sugar

¾ cup water

¾ cup fruity white wine, such as Riesling
(can be nonalcoholic) or hard or soft
cider (see note at left)

2 tablespoons orange liqueur (optional)

PER SERVING:			
Calories	215	FIBER	3.4g
Total Fat	1g	Carbohydrate	47g
Saturated Fat	0g	Protein	1g
Calories from fat	4%	Sodium	4mg

FOR LOWER-FAT COOKIES

Replacing the fat in cookies is trickier than
with cakes and quick breads, so you'll have
to do some experimenting. Replacing ⅔ to
¾ of the fat called for in a recipe with corn
syrup or brown rice syrup often works well.
You can use applesauce as the fat replacer,
but the cookies will be softer; syrup makes
a crispier cookie. The Flaxseed Egg
Replacer (p. 183) works well in cookies as
an egg replacer.

Oat-Coconut Crumble Coffee Cake

Makes 10 servings

This is a lovely moist cake with very little fat—great for a tea or coffee party.

Preheat the oven to 350°F. Combine the oat bran and hot water in a medium bowl and let stand while you oil an 8-inch tube pan or 8-inch square cake pan.

Beat together all of the liquid mixture ingredients, and pour into the oat bran mixture. In a small bowl, mix the dry ingredients well. Mix the Topping ingredients in a small bowl, rubbing the margarine in with your fingers to distribute it well. Set aside.

Add the dry mixture to the bowl with the liquid mixture/oat bran mix and stir just until mixed. If you are using the tube pan, sprinkle the Topping in the bottom of the pan and pour the batter over it. If you are using the square pan, pour in the batter and top evenly with the Topping. Bake 25 minutes, or until cake tester inserted in center comes out clean. Cool on a rack before removing from the pan or slicing.

½ cup oat bran
½ cup plus 2 tablespoons hot water

LIQUID MIXTURE

1 cup sugar
¼ cup water blended with 1 tablespoon flaxseeds (p. 183)
¼ cup smooth applesauce
1 tablespoon oil
½ teaspoon vanilla

DRY MIXTURE

¾ cup whole wheat pastry flour
½ teaspoon baking soda
¾ teaspoon baking powder
½ teaspoon salt
½ teaspoon cinnamon

COCONUT CRUMBLE TOPPING

¼ cup brown sugar
¼ cup unsweetened grated coconut
¼ cup whole wheat flour,
oat flour, or oat bran
1 tablespoon nondairy margarine
½ teaspoon cinnamon

PER SERVING:			
Calories	222	FIBER	3.5g
Total Fat	7g	Carbohydrate	39g
Saturated Fat	4g	Protein	3g
Calories from fat	26%	Sodium	212mg

MATRIMONIAL BARS
or Date Squares

Makes 24 bars

I believe that these are only called Matrimonial Bars here in Canada— I don't know why! But they are very popular, and rightly so. The recipe normally contains 1 cup or more butter, lard, or shortening. This recipe not only features high-fiber flours and dried fruit, but the fat has been significantly cut.

Preheat oven to 375°F and oil a 9 x 13-inch pan.

To make the Filling, simmer all of the ingredients in a heavy pot until the liquid is absorbed and a thick, but not too dry, paste forms, about 5 minutes. Remove from heat.

To make the Crumble, mix the oats, flour, sugar, soy flour, oat bran, baking soda, and salt in a medium bowl. Cut in the margarine or oil until the mixture resembles fine crumbs. Stir in applesauce. (Mixture should remain crumbly.) Pat 2½ cups of the Crumble evenly in the bottom of the prepared pan. Spread the date mixture evenly over the Crumble layer. Top evenly with the rest of the Crumble. Bake 30 minutes. Cool on a rack and cut into 24 squares.

FILLING

3 cups chopped pitted dates

1½ cups water or orange juice

1½ tablespoon lemon juice

Grated rind of 1 orange OR 2 teaspoons vanilla and ½ teaspoon almond extract

CRUMBLE

1½ cups quick oats

1½ cups whole wheat flour

1 cup brown sugar or Sucanat

½ cup soy or chickpea flour

½ cup oat bran

½ teaspoon baking soda

½ teaspoon salt

¼ cup nondairy margarine or oil

½ cup smooth applesauce

CRANBERRY SQUARES: Substitute 4 cups (two 1-pound cans) whole cranberry sauce for the date mixture. If you like, add 1 tablespoon lemon zest. Serve with vanilla nondairy ice cream.

FIG SQUARES: Substitute dried chopped figs for the dates.

PER SERVING: each			
Calories	174	FIBER	4.1g
Total Fat	3g	Carbohydrate	36g
Saturated Fat	1g	Protein	4g
Calories from fat	15%	Sodium	89mg

BISCOTTI DI PRATO
(Almond Biscuits)

makes about 40 biscuits

I have substituted unsweetened smooth applesauce for the eggs, and added a little oil to make up for the fat of egg yolks. This adds soluble fiber in the form of apple pectin. One tablespoon oil makes a fairly hard biscuit; 2-3 tablespoons makes one that can be bitten into easily without dunking.

1½ cups whole wheat pastry flour

1½ cups regular whole wheat flour (can be white whole wheat flour, see p. 37)

1 tablespoon baking powder

½ teaspoon salt

1½ cups sugar

¾ cup smooth unsweetened applesauce

1-3 tablespoons oil

1 teaspoon vanilla

1 tsp. pure almond extract

1½ cups almonds, toasted and chopped (or use half almonds and half hazelnuts)

Preheat the oven to 325°F. Lightly oil 2 cookie sheets (use the double-layer ones, if you have them, or shiny ones, or, if yours are very black, line them with foil).

In a large bowl, whisk together the flours, baking powder, and salt. In a medium bowl, whisk together the sugar, applesauce, oil, and extracts. Stir the sugar mixture into the flour mixture, add the nuts and finish mixing with your hands.

With floured hands, shape the dough into two 3-inch-wide "logs," about ¾-inch thick, with ends squared off. Place these on the cookie sheets. Bake the logs for 25 minutes. Remove the pan and reduce the oven heat to 300°F.

Cool the logs on a rack for 15 minutes. Cut the logs carefully with a sharp knife straight across into ½-inch-wide slices. Place the slices cut-side down on the cookie sheets (you can remove the foil, if using). Bake 5-10 minutes, or until just golden on the bottom. Turn the slices over and cook 5-10 minutes more, or until golden on the bottom. Cool on racks, then store airtight for up to two weeks (or freeze).

CHOCOLATE: Omit 1 cup of the pastry flour and add 1 cup unsweetened Dutch cocoa. If you wish, add 1 packet (½ tablespoon) of espresso powder. This is good with hazelnuts (filberts).

PER SERVING:			
Calories	103	FIBER	1.8g
Total Fat	4g	Carbohydrate	16g
Saturated Fat	0g	Protein	3g
Calories from fat	4%	Sodium	55mg

Fiber-Rich
CHOCOLATE CHIP COOKIES

Makes 4 dozen

A recipe of this size generally has about four times as much fat in it, plus more chocolate chips and nuts. These are crisp and very good!

Preheat the oven to 350°F. Spray 4 cookie sheets with oil from a pump sprayer, or with nonstick spray. Beat the margarine, sugars, flaxseed mixture, milk, and vanilla in a food processor or with an electric mixer until smooth.

In a medium bowl, mix all of the Dry mixture ingredients. Add the sugar mixture and mix well to make a firm dough. With wet hands, roll walnut-size pieces into 48 balls. Place 12 on each cookie sheet, evenly spaced; flatten slightly. Bake 5 minutes. Turn the pans around from front to back, and shift the ones on the lower shelf to the top and vice versa, and bake 5 more minutes. Remove from pans and cool on racks. Store airtight after cooling thoroughly, or freeze.

PER SERVING: each			
Calories	101	FIBER	1.3g
Total Fat	4g	Carbohydrate	15g
Saturated Fat	1g	Protein	2g
Calories from fat	35%	Sodium	76mg

6 tablespoons nondairy margarine

¾ cup sugar

¾ cup brown sugar

½ cup water and 2 tablespoons flaxseeds ground in blender (p. 183)

2 tablespoons nondairy milk

½ tablespoon vanilla OR 3 tablespoons grated orange rind

DRY MIXTURE

3 cups whole wheat pastry flour

¼ cup oat bran

½ tablespoon baking soda

½ teaspoon salt

1 cup semi-sweet mini chocolate chips

½-1 cup chopped walnuts or pecans

ICEBOX COOKIES: Form the dough into 4 logs, wrap in foil and refrigerate. Slice each log into 12 pieces.

CHEWY OATMEAL COOKIES: Omit the oat bran and chocolate chips. Use only 1½ cups whole wheat pastry flour and add 1¾ cups rolled oats. Substitute ⅔ cup dried currants or raisins for the chocolate chips. Oil cookie sheets well; these have a tendency to stick. Bake only 3 minutes after you switch the pans around in the oven. Cool on the cookie sheets for 2 minutes; then carefully loosen and remove to racks to cool. These will be more fragile.

PINEAPPLE-CARROT CAKE

Makes one 10" tube or bundt cake (16 servings)

NOTE: Fat-free, moist cakes should be baked in a tube or bundt pan, so they don't get soggy in the middle.

Preheat the oven to 350°F. Spray a 10-inch nonstick tube pan with nonstick spray. Whisk together the dry mixture ingredients in a medium bowl. Combine the liquid mixture ingredients together in a blender or food processor until smooth. Pour this into the dry ingredients along with the pineapple and carrots. Mix briefly, but well.

Beat the powdered egg replacer and water in a deep, small bowl with an electric mixer or rotary beater until it is softly mounded like beaten egg whites.

Fold this carefully into the cake batter until well-distributed. Smooth the batter into the prepared pan and bake for 15 minutes. Reduce heat to 325°F and bake 30 minutes more, or until the cake tests done with a cake tester. Let cool in the pan 5 minutes, then invert on a rack to cool, covered loosely with a clean tea towel. Sprinkle the cake while still warm with powdered sugar, or, if you prefer a creamy frosting, use Tofu-Cashew Creme Cheeze Frosting (page 178).

COOL COMPLETELY BEFORE CUTTING!

DRY MIXTURE

2 cups wholewheat pastry flour OR
1½ cups wholewheat pastry flour PLUS
½ cup oat flour (rolled oats ground in a DRY blender or food processor)

1 teaspoon baking soda

1 teaspoon ground cinnamon

2 teaspoons baking powder

2 teaspoons salt

LIQUID MIXTURE

1½ cups sugar

¼ cup Flaxseed Egg Replacer (p. 183) OR ¼ cup medium-firm tofu

Juice from ½ (19-ounce) can crushed unsweetened pineapple

1 teaspoon vanilla OR ½ teaspoon EACH lemon and coconut extracts

ADDITIONAL INGREDIENTS

½ (19-ounce) can of crushed unsweetened pineapple, drained (juice used above, with liquid ingredients)

2 cups finely grated carrots

1 tablespoon powdered Ener-G egg replacer mixed with ¼ cup cold water

Powdered sugar (for garnish)

PER SERVING:			
Calories	274	FIBER	4.8g
Total Fat	2g	Carbohydrate	60g
Saturated Fat	0g	Protein	6g
Calories from fat	6%	Sodium	296mg

ALEJANDRO'S PUMPKIN-DATE PUDDING

Makes 6-8 servings

This is a light steamed pudding that my father, Alejandro Urbina, loved. It's easy to make, can be made ahead of time, and is lighter than many Christmas puddings.

To make the pudding, sift together the flour, baking powder, baking soda, and salt in a medium bowl. Mix in the sugar, breadcrumbs, dates, and walnuts. In another bowl, beat together the pumpkin, vanilla, oil, and milk. Stir the pumpkin mixture into the dry ingredients just until mixed well; do not beat. Spoon batter into an oiled 8½ x 4¼-inch loaf pan or a pudding mold, filling ⅔ full. Cover tightly with foil and steam over simmering water in a covered pot 1½ hours. Cool 5 minutes. Loosen sides of pudding with a table knife and invert pudding onto a plate. Serve immediately with Liquor Sauce. To reheat, steam 30 minutes.

To make Liquor Sauce, mix the sugar, cornstarch, salt, and water in a small saucepan. Stir constantly until it comes to a boil. Reduce heat and simmer 5 minutes. Remove from heat and add vanilla, whiskey, and margarine if desired. Serve hot.

PUDDING

1¼ cups whole wheat pastry flour

1 teaspoon baking powder

1 teaspoon baking soda

½ teaspoon salt

1 cup sugar

½ cup soft light-textured, 100% whole wheat breadcrumbs

1 cup chopped pitted dates

1 cup chopped walnuts

1 cup canned pumpkin

1 teaspoon vanilla

1½ tablespoons oil or melted nondairy margarine

½ cup nondairy milk

LIQUOR SAUCE

¾ cup brown sugar

1 tablespoon cornstarch

Pinch of salt

1 cup water

1 tablespoon vanilla

3 tablespoons whiskey, brandy, or dark rum

2-4 tablespoons nondairy margarine (optional)

PER SERVING:			
Calories	568	FIBER	6.5g
Total Fat	20g	Carbohydrate	91g
Saturated Fat	3g	Protein	7g
Calories from fat	31%	Sodium	451mg

Rustic Rhubarb Cake

Makes 16-20 servings

This is one of our old family favorites—easy and always appreciated.

Preheat oven to 350°F. Oil a 9 x 13-inch cake pan.

Whisk together all of the Dry Mixture ingredients in a medium mixing bowl. Stir in the rhubarb. In a blender, blend all of the Wet Mixture ingredients until smooth. Mix the Wet Mixture into Dry Mixture, stirring as briefly as possible. Spread into prepared pan.

Mix the Topping ingredients together in a small bowl. Sprinkle the Topping evenly over the cake. Bake 35 minutes or until cake tester inserted in center comes out clean.

Cool on a rack and cut into squares.

DRY MIXTURE

1¾ cups whole wheat pastry flour
PLUS ¼ cup oat bran OR
2 cups whole wheat flour

1 teaspoon baking powder

½ teaspoon baking soda

½ teaspoon salt

¼ teaspoon ground allspice

2 cups chopped fresh or frozen unthawed rhubarb

WET MIXTURE

⅓ cup smooth unsweetened applesauce

3 tablespoons oil

1 cup sugar

⅞ cup nondairy milk

TOPPING

½ cup brown sugar

1 teaspoon cinnamon

¼ cup chopped walnuts, pecans, or sunflower seeds

PER SERVING:			
Calories	151	FIBER	1.7g
Total Fat	4g	Carbohydrate	28g
Saturated Fat	0g	Protein	3g
Calories from fat	23%	Sodium	119mg

Carrot Fruitcake

Makes two 3 x 6-inch loaves plus one 8 x 4-inch loaf (32-34 slices)

This fruitcake is rich-tasting and moist, and yet it is not full of eggs, butter, or worse yet, suet, like many traditional recipes. I based it on an old wartime boiled raisin cake.

For the Boiled Mixture, bring all of the ingredients to a boil in a medium saucepan. Reduce heat and simmer 10 minutes. Set aside to cool. Preheat oven to 300°F. Lightly oil two 3 x 6-inch loaf pans and one 8 x 4-inch loaf pan; line bottom of pans with parchment paper or waxed paper.

In a large bowl mix all of the Dry Ingredients. Add the cooled Boiled Mixture and the Dried Fruits and Nuts. Mix well and spoon into oiled pans. Bake the small loaves 45 minutes and the large loaf 60 minutes. Invert on racks to cool. Carefully peel off the paper.

NOTE: You can serve this fruitcake immediately after cooling, but to store, wrap the cooled loaves in liquor-soaked cheesecloth, and keep them for several weeks. Or wrap in foil, in which case they should be frozen after 10 days.

BOILED MIXTURE

1½ cups water or apple juice, (½ cup can be rum or brandy)

1 cup grated unpeeled carrots

1 cup raisins

1 cup brown sugar or Sucanat

¼ cup molasses

1 teaspoon ground cinnamon

1 teaspoon salt

¼ teaspoon ground cloves

¼ cup oil or nondairy margarine

DRY INGREDIENTS

1½ cups whole wheat flour (not pastry flour)

½ cup wheat germ

1 teaspoon baking soda

DRIED FRUITS AND NUTS

1 cup whole or chopped mixed dried fruits

1 cup whole or chopped pitted dates

1 cup dried currants

½ cup chopped walnuts

1 cup whole shelled mixed nuts

PER SERVING:

Calories	132	FIBER	2.4g
Total Fat	3g	Carbohydrate	25g
Saturated Fat	0g	Protein	2g
Calories from fat	20%	Sodium	111mg

FUDGEY LIGHT BROWNIES

Makes 16 servings

These are healthful and low-fat, plus they have a respectable fiber content and they are delicious!

Preheat oven to 350°F. In a small saucepan, melt the margarine and 3 tablespoons water gently over medium heat OR in a medium-small microwave-proof bowl in the microwave 1 minute. (If using oil instead of margarine, mix oil with 3 tablespoons hot water.) Stir in the sugar until dissolved. Stir in the cocoa, vanilla, and espresso powder. Set aside.

Place the ¼ cup water, flaxseeds, and Egg Replacer in a blender. Blend on high for several minutes, until the mixture resembles slightly beaten egg whites. Fold into the cocoa mixture.

In a small bowl, mix together the flour, baking powder, salt, and nuts. Add the flour mixture to the cocoa mixture and stir briefly.

Oil a 9-inch square or 7 x 11-inch rectangular baking pan. Spread batter into prepared pan. Bake the 9-inch pan about 20 minutes, the 7 x 11-inch about 17 minutes. Cool completely on a wire rack before cutting.

3 tablespoons nondairy margarine or 3 tablespoons oil

3 tablespoons water

1 cup brown sugar or Sucanat

½ cup Dutch (dark) unsweetened cocoa powder

2 teaspoons vanilla

1 tablespoon espresso powder or instant coffee or coffee substitute granules (see Variation below) AND/OR 1 tablespoon grated orange zest

¼ cup water

1 tablespoon flaxseeds

1 tablespoon Ener-G Egg Replacer

½ cup regular whole wheat flour (not pastry flour)

½ teaspoon baking powder

¼ teaspoon salt

¼ to ½ cup chopped nuts, toasted briefly

VARIATION: If you want coffee flavor but have no espresso powder or instant coffee granules, use strong liquid coffee or espresso for the 3 tablespoons water AND for the ¼ cup water that you blend with the flaxseed and Egg Replacer.

PER SERVING:

Calories	118	FIBER	1.6g
Total Fat	5g	Carbohydrate	19g
Saturated Fat	1g	Protein	2g
Calories from fat	38%	Sodium	83mg

TROPICAL DELIGHT CAKE

Makes 12-16 servings

This is a new version of a recipe from the La Leche League International official cookbook, Whole Foods for the Whole Family *(NAL Books), for which I was an Associate Editor. It makes a nutty, fruity special occasion cake.*

Preheat oven to 350°F. Oil and flour a 10-inch tube pan.

Combine the flaxseed mixture, sugar, and oil and blend well. Add pineapple and juice and blend briefly.

In a medium bowl, whisk the Dry mixture ingredients. Stir in the dates, nuts, and coconut. Add the liquid mixture and stir briefly. Pour into prepared pan. Bake 35-40 minutes. Cool and frost with Banana-Nut Creme Cheeze Frosting (page 179).

WET MIXTURE

½ cup water and 2 tablespoons flaxseeds ground in blender (p. 183)

¾-1 cup sugar

2 tablespoons oil

1 (19-ounce) can crushed pineapple (unsweetened) with juice

DRY MIXTURE

2 cups whole wheat pastry flour

1 teaspoon baking soda

1 teaspoon baking powder

½ teaspoon salt

2 tablespoons soymilk powder or rice milk powder

¼ cup wheat germ

1 cup diced pitted dates

¾ cup chopped nuts

½ cup unsweetened shredded coconut

PER SERVING:

Calories	306	FIBER	5.6g
Total Fat	13g	Carbohydrate	46g
Saturated Fat	5g	Protein	6g
Calories from fat	38%	Sodium	202mg

Pear Upside-Down Cake

Makes 16 servings

Preheat the oven to 350°F.

In a 10-inch cast-iron skillet, melt the margarine in the oven while it preheats. When the margarine is melted, spread the brown sugar evenly over it. Sprinkle with the nuts. Arrange pears cut-side up in pan. Cut a little slice off the round bottom of the pears so they sit evenly in the pan.

Pour gingerbread batter over pears and spread evenly. Bake 45 minutes until cake tester inserted in center comes out clean. Loosen edges with a butter knife and invert carefully on a large plate. Scrape off any syrup left behind in the pan and spread on pears. Cool on a rack.

¼ cup nondairy margarine

1 cup brown sugar

½-1 cup chopped walnuts or pecans

6 medium-large ripe pears, peeled, cored, and halved, OR 12 canned unsweetened pear halves

1 recipe Whole Wheat Gingerbread batter (unbaked; p. 179)

PER SERVING:

Calories	315	FIBER	4.3g
Total Fat	10g	Carbohydrate	56g
Saturated Fat	1g	Protein	4g
Calories from fat	28%	Sodium	188mg

Tofu-Cashew Creme Cheeze Frosting

Makes 2½ cups (enough for a 2-3 layer cake)

Crumble the tofu into a clean tea towel and gather up the ends. Twist and squeeze repeatedly until the tofu is as dry as possible. Beat all of the frosting ingredients in a food processor until very smooth. Refrigerate while the cake is being made. Check the frosting when you take the cake out of the oven. If it is too firm to spread, leave it at room temperature while the cake cools. Refrigerate the frosted cake.

2 (12.3-ounce) boxes extra-firm lite SILKEN tofu (squeezed as noted above)

⅔ cup raw cashew pieces, ground fine in a mini-chopper or coffee/spice mill

⅓ cup light maple syrup

3 tablespoons plus 1 teaspoon lemon juice

1¼ teaspoons vanilla

1 teaspoon salt

PER SERVING: 2½ tablespoons

Calories	69	FIBER	0.5g
Total Fat	3g	Carbohydrate	7g
Saturated Fat	1g	Protein	4g
Calories from fat	39%	Sodium	176mg

FROSTING VARIATIONS

LEMON CREME CHEEZE FROSTING: Use ¼ cup lemon juice, and use 1 teaspoon vanilla. Add 1 tablespoon grated lemon zest (preferably organic).

BANANA-NUT OR COCONUT CREME CHEEZE FROSTING: Add 1 small ripe mashed banana to the processed mixture and fold or pulse in ¼ cup minced toasted walnuts, pecans, or unsweetened coconut flakes.

WHOLE WHEAT GINGERBREAD

Makes 16 servings

Moist, dark, and spicy—also low-fat and fiber-rich.

Preheat oven to 350°F. Oil and flour a 9-inch square pan.

Add all of the Wet Mixture ingredients with flaxseed mixture in blender and blend well.

In a medium bowl, mix all of the Dry Mixture ingredients well. Pour in the Wet Mixture and mix briefly. Spread the batter in the prepared pan and bake 25-35 minutes, until cake tester inserted in center comes out clean. Serve warm or cool.

WET MIXTURE

1 cup dark molasses

½ tablespoon lemon juice plus soymilk or other nondairy milk to make ½ cup

½ cup sugar (dark or light) or Sucanat

⅓ cup smooth applesauce

2 tablespoons oil*

¼ cup water and 2 tablespoons flaxseeds ground in blender (p. 183)

DRY MIXTURE

2 cups whole wheat pastry flour

1 tablespoon ground ginger

1 teaspoon baking soda

1 teaspoon cinnamon

½ teaspoon salt

½ teaspoon allspice

*Olive oil works well in this recipe.

PER SERVING:			
Calories	164	FIBER	2.4g
Total Fat	3g	Carbohydrate	32g
Saturated Fat	0g	Protein	3g
Calories from fat	16%	Sodium	156mg

"Sour Creme" Coffee Cake

Makes 16 servings

Preheat oven to 350°F. Oil and flour a 10-inch bundt or tube cake pan.

Add all of the Wet Mixture ingredients with flaxseed mixture in blender and blend well. Pour into a medium mixing bowl.

In a separate bowl, whisk together all of the Dry Mixture ingredients; set aside.

In the blender (no need to wash it after blending the Wet Mixture), blend the "Sour Creme" ingredients until very smooth.

Add the Dry Mixture and the "Sour Creme" alternately to the Wet Mixture, starting and ending with the Dry Mixture and stirring as little as possible.

Mix the Topping ingredients well in a small bowl. Sprinkle half of the Topping into the bottom of the prepared pan. Top with half the batter. Sprinkle the rest of the Topping over that and end with the remaining batter.

Bake 45 minutes or until cake tester inserted in center comes out clean. Cool on a rack 5 minutes, then loosen it carefully with a butter knife and invert carefully onto a serving plate. Cool on a rack.

WET MIXTURE

⅓ cup smooth, unsweetened applesauce

3 tablespoons oil

¼ cup soymilk

1 cup sugar

1 teaspoon vanilla extract

¼ cup water and 1 tablespoon flaxseeds ground in blender (p. 183)

DRY MIXTURE

1 cup whole wheat pastry flour

¾ cup unbleached flour

¼ cup oat bran

1 teaspoon each baking powder and soda

½ teaspoon salt

"SOUR CREME"

½ cup medium-firm tofu OR firm or extra-firm SILKEN tofu

½ cup soymilk

1 tablespoon lemon juice

TOPPING

1 cup chopped walnuts or pecans

⅓ cup nondairy margarine, melted

⅔ cup brown sugar

1 teaspoon cinnamon

PER SERVING:			
Calories	239	FIBER	2.2g
Total Fat	11g	Carbohydrate	34g
Saturated Fat	1g	Protein	4g
Calories from fat	41%	Sodium	194mg

BLACKBERRY APPLE CRUMBLE

Makes 6-8 servings

The British are fond of combining apples and blackberries in desserts—it makes sense, since they are both harvested in the early fall and they complement each other beautifully! (A "crumble" is the British term for what we call a "crisp.")

Preheat the oven to 375°F. Combine the apples, blackberries, flour, and sugar gently in a 9 to 10-inch round or square baking pan. Rub the topping ingredients together in a small bowl with your fingertips until crumbly. Sprinkle over the fruit. Bake 40 minutes. Serve warm with your favorite nondairy vanilla frozen dessert, nondairy whipped topping, or organic nondairy coffee creamer.

CRANAPPLE CRISP: Substitute 3 cups cranberries for the blackberries. Use ½ cup sugar.

APPLE RAISIN CRISP: Use 6-8 apples and ½ cup raisins instead of the berries. Use ¼ cup sugar.

3 medium-sized tart apples (about 1 pound), unpeeled, cored, and cut into ¼-inch slices

3 pints ripe blackberries

1 tablespoon unbleached flour

¼-½ cup sugar

TOPPING

⅔ cup rolled oats

⅓ cup whole wheat flour

⅓ cup brown sugar

1 teaspoon cinnamon

3 tablespoons oil or nondairy margarine

½ cup chopped nuts

PER SERVING:

Calories	338	FIBER	9.9g
Total Fat	13g	Carbohydrate	56g
Saturated Fat	1g	Protein	5g
Calories from fat	34%	Sodium	5mg

APPLESAUCE DATE CAKE

Makes 12 servings

Applesauce replaces the eggs and butter in this deliciously moist cake. (It's even better the next day!)

Preheat the oven to 350°F. Oil and flour a 9-inch square cake pan.

In a small saucepan, slowly warm the applesauce with the orange juice.

Mix the flour, oat bran, sugar, salt, and spices in a medium bowl. Add the dates and mix well. Scoop into the prepared pan, smooth the top and bake 10 minutes. Reduce the heat to 325°F and bake about 25-30 minutes more, or until cake tester inserted in center comes out clean. Cool thoroughly on a rack and cut into 12 bars.

I cup smooth unsweetened applesauce

3 tablespoons orange juice

I cup whole wheat pastry flour

¼ cup oat bran

½ cup granulated or brown sugar

½ teaspoon cinnamon

¼ teaspoon salt

⅛ teaspoon ground nutmeg

⅛ teaspoon ground allspice

I teaspoon baking soda

I cup chopped pitted dates

PER SERVING:

Calories	127	FIBER	3g
Total Fat	1g	Carbohydrate	30g
Saturated Fat	0g	Protein	2g
Calories from fat	7%	Sodium	328mg

FLAXSEED—THE HIGH-FIBER EGG REPLACER

When blended with water, high-fiber flaxseeds make a good egg substitute in some baked goods when only an egg or two is called for. Simply blend 1 tablespoon raw flaxseed (frozen is fine) with ¼ cup water for each egg and use it immediately in your recipe (you can use warm water if the seeds are frozen). This can be done in a blender or with an immersion blender (both of these work better than a food processor for this).

IMPORTANT NOTE: The blending takes several minutes and gets thick and viscous like egg white. Do not stop blending until it reaches this point. If you don't want the flecks of brown skin to show in your mixture (not a problem, unless the mixture you are adding it to is very white), you can strain it through a fine sieve or cheesecloth, but this is usually not necessary.

You may want to experiment with adding about ½ tablespoon of powdered egg replacer per ¼ cup of flaxseed egg replacer in some recipes, to compensate for the leavening power of the egg, as well (see the brownie recipe on page 176 for an example of this). I find that eggless doughs often taste a little flat, so I usually add a little more salt, too.

NOTE: I find that this flaxseed egg replacer can be a bit drying to some baked goods (flaxseeds suck up liquid), so I use it judiciously, not for everything.

BEAN COOKING TIMES

Use 3 cups of water for each cup of dried beans

Bean	Soaked, open kettle	No soak and pressure cook	Soak and pressure cook	Yield per 2 cups dry
Aduki	30 min.	15 min.	5-10 min.	6⅔
Anasazi	60 min.	25 min.	15 min.	5
Black	90 min.	30-35 min.	20 min.	5
Black-eyed peas	25 min.	10 min.	5-8 min.	4¾
Chickpea	4½ hrs.	35 min.	25 min.	5
Great Northern	90 min.	25 min.	20 min.	5
Kidney	35-40 min.	30 min.	15-20 min.	4½
Lentil, brown*	20-25 min.	**	**	5
Lentil, red*	20-25 min.	**	**	3½
Lima, baby	30 min.	10-15 min.	8 min.	4
Navy	35-40 min.	25 min.	15 min.	5
Pinto	90 min.	35-40 min.	20-25 min.	5
Soybeans	**	60 min.	45 min.	4
Split Peas*	75-90 min.	7 min.	**	4

Notes:

*It is not necessary to presoak lentils and split peas.

**Do not use this method for these beans.

GLOSSARY

Many of these products can be found in larger supermarkets, natural food stores, or Chinese, Indian, or other ethnic foods stores.

Besan or chickpea flour: Flour made by grinding chickpeas; found in some large supermarkets, health food stores, East Asian, Middle Eastern, and Mediterranean markets.

Bulghur: Wheat kernels that have been boiled, dried, and cracked to make a grain that cooks in just 10 to 15 minutes. Bulghur is an essential ingredient in many Middle Eastern dishes.

Chile chipotle (CHEE-lay chee-POHT-lay): Smoked jalapeño chilies. You can buy them dried or in cans; often found in Mexican markets or large supermarkets.

Filé powder (FEE-lay or fih-LAY): Dried, powdered sassafras leaves, often used in the South to thicken gumbos. The powder gets stringy when it's heated, so add it only after you've removed the gumbo from the heat source. Filé also doesn't reheat well, so add it only to the gumbo that you're planning to eat right away.

Flaxseeds (linseeds): Small brown or golden seeds that can be ground in a spice mill, coffee grinder, or blender, a little at a time and used as an egg substitute in baking (see page 183).

Garlic granules: Ground, dried garlic, a better quality and often easier to use than garlic powder.

Gluten powder, instant: Also known as vital wheat gluten, it is mixed with water or broth to form a stiff dough, then simmered to produce a variety of meat substitutes.

Isolated soy protein powder (or soy protein isolate): Pure soy protein powder (fiber-free) processed from defatted soy flakes. This powder is bland and highly digestible, easy to add to shakes and other recipes, and available in health food stores, supplement stores, and by mail order.

Liquid smoke: A natural hickory smoke flavoring useful for replacing the flavor of ham and bacon, especially in bean dishes.

Marmite (*See* yeast extract)

Masa harina: A flour made from hominy and used to make corn tortillas and tamales, and available in large supermarkets or Hispanic markets.

Miso: A Japanese fermented soybean and grain paste, usually made with rice or barley, which is used as a soup base and flavoring (similar to bouillon paste or cubes). It is salty, but highly nutritious, and valued for its digestive properties. Unpasteurized miso contains beneficial bacteria similar to that in yogurt, so it should be added to cooked foods at the last minute and not brought to the boiling point. It can be found in a number of varieties—dark, light, yellow, sweet, etc.

Nondairy margarine: Check the label for milk products (whey, etc.). The brand I like the best is Earth Balance Natural Buttery Spread, which is nonhydrogenated, made from expeller-pressed oils, has no GMOs, and really tastes good.

Soy Parmesan: I use Soymage 100 percent dairy-free Parmesan substitute, which is tofu-based and calcium-enriched. It is quite delicious and will keep refrigerated for 6 months, and frozen for longer.

Nutritional yeast flakes: Nutritional yeast is NOT the same thing as brewer's yeast or baking yeast. Nutritional yeast flakes have a cheesey taste when used alone, but they can also add an "egg-yolk" flavor to tofu egg substitutes, and a chickeny flavor when used with soy sauce. Red Star Vegetarian Support Formula Flakes are especially good tasting.

Powdered egg replacer: Ener-G egg replacer is a powder made from potato and tapioca starches. Half a tablespoon of the powder beaten with 2 tablespoons cold water replaces one egg. There are other brands on the market, but, in my experience, this is the best.

Quinoa (KEEN-wah): This ancient staple of the Incas is a grain which cooks quickly and has a mild flavor and a delightful, slightly crunchy texture. Rinse quinoa before using to remove its bitter natural coating.

Seitan (say-tan): Seitan (the Japanese word for cooked, seasoned wheat gluten) is used as a meat substitute because of its chewy texture. It is available in the refrigerator section of

most natural food stores (or as a packaged mix to make your own), and in many canned versions in Asian grocery stores (such as mun chai'ya, or vegetarian "roast duck").

Soba: Japanese buckwheat noodles.

Spelt: A relative of wheat, this grain contains gluten, although it's tolerated by many people who are allergic to gluten.

Steam-fry: Sautéeing or sir-frying without fat. Use a lightly oiled pan and one or two tablespoons of liquid (water, broth, or wine), adding JUST ENOUGH liquid to keep the vegetables from sticking to the bottom of the pan.

Sucanat: An unprocessed sugar made from granulated, dehydrated sugar cane juice and can be used like white or light brown sugar.

Tahini: Ground sesame butter made from hulled sesame seeds. Using just a little adds a wonderful richness to dishes.

Tempeh (tem-pay): A cultured product native to Indonesia made from either soybeans or other beans and grains. It has a slightly nutty flavor and firm texture that many people like as a meat or poultry substitute, especially in stir-fry dishes. It should be kept frozen after purchasing and should be fried or steamed if it is added to a dish for which no other cooking is required.

Textured soy or vegetable protein: A meat substitute made from defatted soy flour. It can be found in a variety of textures and shapes. It is used primarily in a granular form, which is used in place of ground meat, or in chunk form, which is great in stews and kebabs. Generally, you can hydrate textured soy by soaking or simmering it in equal parts water or broth.

Tofu: A soft "cheese" made from soymilk that is curded with mineral salts and then drained and pressed into different textures. It is used widely in Asian cooking and vegetarian cooking. This isoflavone-rich soyfood is extremely versatile, taking on flavors easily, and can be used to substitute for dairy products, meat, poultry, seafood, and eggs. Soft tofu is good for drinks and desserts; regular or medium-firm tofu (Japanese style), firm tofu (Chinese style), or extra-firm tofu (sometimes known as pressed) are excellent for marinating, stir-frying, and making kebabs.

Udon: Thick Japanese wheat noodles.

Vegemite (*See* yeast extract)

Vital wheat gluten (*See* gluten powder)

Wheat berries, whole wheat berries, or wheat kernels: Wheat kernels that have been stripped only of their inedible outer hulls. Ground, they make wholewheat flour. They are available in health food stores and in bulk in some supermarkets.

Yeast extract (also, Marmite, Vegemite, etc.): This dark, salty paste with a "beefy" flavor is popular as a spread in England and Australia. It also adds a rich, dark flavor to meatless dishes.

SOURCES FOR HARD-TO-FIND INGREDIENTS

The Mail Order Catalog for Healthy Eating
P.O. Box 180
Summertown, TN 38483
1-800-695-2241
www.healthy-eating.com
Textured soy products and other meat substitutes, seitan, egg and dairy substitutes, nutritional yeast, flaxseeds, soy Parmesan, and other natural food products.

To buy Marmite online;
BuyMarmite@www.goodwoods.com

To buy Vegemite online:
http://www.thekiwishop.com/index.html

Seventh Day Adventist book and food stores: Sell vegetarian and vegan foods as well as books and are often in rural areas. They carry kosher gel, vegetarian meat substitutes, yeast extract (Savorex) and many other foods, some hard to find.
To find a store near you, call:
1-800-765-6955).

CANADA:

Online natural food and organic shopping (from BC):
http://qualityorganics.com/

This store isn't online and doesn't have a catalog, but they say they'll deliver phone orders anywhere in Canada!
Choices Market Ltd
2627 West 16th Ave
Vancouver, B.C. V6K 3C2
(604) 736-0009

INDEX

BOOK PUBLISHING COMPANY

since 1974—books that educate, inspire, and empower

To find your favorite vegetarian and soyfood products online, visit:

www.healthy-eating.com

Also by Bryanna Clark Grogan

Authentic Chinese Cuisine
978-1-57067-101-2 $14.95

Dairy-Free & Delicious
Brenda Davis, R.D
recipes by Bryanna Grogan
& Joanne Stepaniak
978-1-57067-124-1 $14.95

Nonna's Italian Kitchen
978-1-57067-055-8 $15.95

Local Bounty
Devra Gartenstein
978-1-57067-219-4 $17.95

More Fabulous Beans
Barb Bloomfield
978-1-57067-146-3 $14.95

*Tofu Cookery 25th
Anniversary Edition*
Louise Hagler
978-1-57067-220-0 $21.95

Purchase these vegetarian cookbooks from your local
bookstore or natural foods store, or you can buy them
directly from: Book Publishing Co., P.O. Box 99,
Summertown, TN 38483
1-800-695-2241

Please include $3.95
per book for shipping
and handling.